Principal
administrative analyst :
©2018.
33305242618019
ca 12/12/19

THIS IS YOUR **PASSBOOK®** FOR ...

PRINCIPAL ADMINISTRATIVE ANALYST

COPYRIGHT NOTICE

This book is SOLELY intended for, is sold ONLY to, and its use is RESTRICTED to individual, bona fide applicants or candidates who qualify by virtue of having seriously filed applications for appropriate license, certificate, professional and/or promotional advancement, higher school matriculation, scholarship, or other legitimate requirements of educational and/or governmental authorities.

This book is NOT intended for use, class instruction, tutoring, training, duplication, copying, reprinting, excerption, or adaptation, etc., by:

1) Other publishers
2) Proprietors and/or Instructors of «Coaching» and/or Preparatory Courses
3) Personnel and/or Training Divisions of commercial, industrial, and governmental organizations
4) Schools, colleges, or universities and/or their departments and staffs, including teachers and other personnel
5) Testing Agencies or Bureaus
6) Study groups which seek by the purchase of a single volume to copy and/or duplicate and/or adapt this material for use by the group as a whole without having purchased individual volumes for each of the members of the group
7) Et al.

Such persons would be in violation of appropriate Federal and State statutes.

PROVISION OF LICENSING AGREEMENTS. — Recognized educational, commercial, industrial, and governmental institutions and organizations, and others legitimately engaged in educational pursuits, including training, testing, and measurement activities, may address request for a licensing agreement to the copyright owners, who will determine whether, and under what conditions, including fees and charges, the materials in this book may be used them. In other words, a licensing facility exists for the legitimate use of the material in this book on other than an individual basis. However, it is asseverated and affirmed here that the material in this book CANNOT be used without the receipt of the express permission of such a licensing agreement from the Publishers. Inquiries re licensing should be addressed to the company, attention rights and permissions department.

All rights reserved, including the right of reproduction in whole or in part, in any form or by any means, electronic or mechanical, including photocopying, recording, or by any information storage and retrieval system, without permission in writing from the Publisher.

Copyright © 2018 by

212 Michael Drive, Syosset, NY 11791
(516) 921-8888 • www.passbooks.com
E-mail: info@passbooks.com

PUBLISHED IN THE UNITED STATES OF AMERICA

PASSBOOK® SERIES

THE *PASSBOOK® SERIES* has been created to prepare applicants and candidates for the ultimate academic battlefield – the examination room.

At some time in our lives, each and every one of us may be required to take an examination – for validation, matriculation, admission, qualification, registration, certification, or licensure.

Based on the assumption that every applicant or candidate has met the basic formal educational standards, has taken the required number of courses, and read the necessary texts, the *PASSBOOK® SERIES* furnishes the one special preparation which may assure passing with confidence, instead of failing with insecurity. Examination questions – together with answers – are furnished as the basic vehicle for study so that the mysteries of the examination and its compounding difficulties may be eliminated or diminished by a sure method.

This book is meant to help you pass your examination provided that you qualify and are serious in your objective.

The entire field is reviewed through the huge store of content information which is succinctly presented through a provocative and challenging approach – the question-and-answer method.

A climate of success is established by furnishing the correct answers at the end of each test.

You soon learn to recognize types of questions, forms of questions, and patterns of questioning. You may even begin to anticipate expected outcomes.

You perceive that many questions are repeated or adapted so that you can gain acute insights, which may enable you to score many sure points.

You learn how to confront new questions, or types of questions, and to attack them confidently and work out the correct answers.

You note objectives and emphases, and recognize pitfalls and dangers, so that you may make positive educational adjustments.

Moreover, you are kept fully informed in relation to new concepts, methods, practices, and directions in the field.

You discover that you arre actually taking the examination all the time: you are preparing for the examination by "taking" an examination, not by reading extraneous and/or supererogatory textbooks.

In short, this PASSBOOK®, used directedly, should be an important factor in helping you to pass your test.

PRINCIPAL ADMINISTRATIVE ANALYST

DUTIES

Directs, plans, supervises, and performs technical work in personnel management. Supervises professional work in reviewing budgeting requirements and contracts; preparation and conduct of management and administrative surveys; evaluation of organizational structures, policies, programs, projects, and contracts. May supervise subordinate staff. Performs related work.

SCOPE OF THE EXAMINATION

The written test may involve questions concerning, and the ability to analyze, problems in the following areas:

1. Management and methods;
2. Organization and structures;
3. Methods, tools, and techniques involved in personnel administration;
4. Budgeting and fiscal control;
5. Administrative techniques;
6. Research techniques;
7. Report writing techniques; and
8. Administrative supervision.

HOW TO TAKE A TEST

I. YOU MUST PASS AN EXAMINATION

A. WHAT EVERY CANDIDATE SHOULD KNOW

Examination applicants often ask us for help in preparing for the written test. What can I study in advance? What kinds of questions will be asked? How will the test be given? How will the papers be graded?

As an applicant for a civil service examination, you may be wondering about some of these things. Our purpose here is to suggest effective methods of advance study and to describe civil service examinations.

Your chances for success on this examination can be increased if you know how to prepare. Those "pre-examination jitters" can be reduced if you know what to expect. You can even experience an adventure in good citizenship if you know why civil service exams are given.

B. WHY ARE CIVIL SERVICE EXAMINATIONS GIVEN?

Civil service examinations are important to you in two ways. As a citizen, you want public jobs filled by employees who know how to do their work. As a job seeker, you want a fair chance to compete for that job on an equal footing with other candidates. The best-known means of accomplishing this two-fold goal is the competitive examination.

Exams are widely publicized throughout the nation. They may be administered for jobs in federal, state, city, municipal, town or village governments or agencies.

Any citizen may apply, with some limitations, such as the age or residence of applicants. Your experience and education may be reviewed to see whether you meet the requirements for the particular examination. When these requirements exist, they are reasonable and applied consistently to all applicants. Thus, a competitive examination may cause you some uneasiness now, but it is your privilege and safeguard.

C. HOW ARE CIVIL SERVICE EXAMS DEVELOPED?

Examinations are carefully written by trained technicians who are specialists in the field known as "psychological measurement," in consultation with recognized authorities in the field of work that the test will cover. These experts recommend the subject matter areas or skills to be tested; only those knowledges or skills important to your success on the job are included. The most reliable books and source materials available are used as references. Together, the experts and technicians judge the difficulty level of the questions.

Test technicians know how to phrase questions so that the problem is clearly stated. Their ethics do not permit "trick" or "catch" questions. Questions may have been tried out on sample groups, or subjected to statistical analysis, to determine their usefulness.

Written tests are often used in combination with performance tests, ratings of training and experience, and oral interviews. All of these measures combine to form the best-known means of finding the right person for the right job.

II. HOW TO PASS THE WRITTEN TEST

A. NATURE OF THE EXAMINATION

To prepare intelligently for civil service examinations, you should know how they differ from school examinations you have taken. In school you were assigned certain definite pages to read or subjects to cover. The examination questions were quite detailed and usually emphasized memory. Civil service exams, on the other hand, try to discover your present ability to perform the duties of a position, plus your potentiality to learn these duties. In other words, a civil service exam attempts to predict how successful you will be. Questions cover such a broad area that they cannot be as minute and detailed as school exam questions.

In the public service similar kinds of work, or positions, are grouped together in one "class." This process is known as *position-classification.* All the positions in a class are paid according to the salary range for that class. One class title covers all of these positions, and they are all tested by the same examination.

B. FOUR BASIC STEPS

1) Study the announcement

How, then, can you know what subjects to study? Our best answer is: "Learn as much as possible about the class of positions for which you've applied." The exam will test the knowledge, skills and abilities needed to do the work.

Your most valuable source of information about the position you want is the official exam announcement. This announcement lists the training and experience qualifications. Check these standards and apply only if you come reasonably close to meeting them.

The brief description of the position in the examination announcement offers some clues to the subjects which will be tested. Think about the job itself. Review the duties in your mind. Can you perform them, or are there some in which you are rusty? Fill in the blank spots in your preparation.

Many jurisdictions preview the written test in the exam announcement by including a section called "Knowledge and Abilities Required," "Scope of the Examination," or some similar heading. Here you will find out specifically what fields will be tested.

2) Review your own background

Once you learn in general what the position is all about, and what you need to know to do the work, ask yourself which subjects you already know fairly well and which need improvement. You may wonder whether to concentrate on improving your strong areas or on building some background in your fields of weakness. When the announcement has specified "some knowledge" or "considerable knowledge," or has used adjectives like "beginning principles of..." or "advanced ... methods," you can get a clue as to the number and difficulty of questions to be asked in any given field. More questions, and hence broader coverage, would be included for those subjects which are more important in the work. Now weigh your strengths and weaknesses against the job requirements and prepare accordingly.

3) Determine the level of the position

Another way to tell how intensively you should prepare is to understand the level of the job for which you are applying. Is it the entering level? In other words, is this the position in which beginners in a field of work are hired? Or is it an intermediate or advanced level? Sometimes this is indicated by such words as "Junior" or "Senior" in the class title. Other jurisdictions use Roman numerals to designate the level – Clerk I, Clerk II, for example. The word "Supervisor" sometimes appears in the title. If the level is not indicated by the title, check the description of duties. Will you be working under very close supervision, or will you have responsibility for independent decisions in this work?

4) Choose appropriate study materials

Now that you know the subjects to be examined and the relative amount of each subject to be covered, you can choose suitable study materials. For beginning level jobs, or even advanced ones, if you have a pronounced weakness in some aspect of your training, read a modern, standard textbook in that field. Be sure it is up to date and has general coverage. Such books are normally available at your library, and the librarian will be glad to help you locate one. For entry-level positions, questions of appropriate difficulty are chosen – neither highly advanced questions, nor those too simple. Such questions require careful thought but not advanced training.

If the position for which you are applying is technical or advanced, you will read more advanced, specialized material. If you are already familiar with the basic principles of your field, elementary textbooks would waste your time. Concentrate on advanced textbooks and technical periodicals. Think through the concepts and review difficult problems in your field.

These are all general sources. You can get more ideas on your own initiative, following these leads. For example, training manuals and publications of the government agency which employs workers in your field can be useful, particularly for technical and professional positions. A letter or visit to the government department involved may result in more specific study suggestions, and certainly will provide you with a more definite idea of the exact nature of the position you are seeking.

III. KINDS OF TESTS

Tests are used for purposes other than measuring knowledge and ability to perform specified duties. For some positions, it is equally important to test ability to make adjustments to new situations or to profit from training. In others, basic mental abilities not dependent on information are essential. Questions which test these things may not appear as pertinent to the duties of the position as those which test for knowledge and information. Yet they are often highly important parts of a fair examination. For very general questions, it is almost impossible to help you direct your study efforts. What we can do is to point out some of the more common of these general abilities needed in public service positions and describe some typical questions.

1) General information

Broad, general information has been found useful for predicting job success in some kinds of work. This is tested in a variety of ways, from vocabulary lists to questions about current events. Basic background in some field of work, such as sociology or economics, may be sampled in a group of questions. Often these are principles which have become familiar to most persons through exposure rather than through formal training. It is difficult to advise you how to study for these questions; being alert to the world around you is our best suggestion.

2) Verbal ability

An example of an ability needed in many positions is verbal or language ability. Verbal ability is, in brief, the ability to use and understand words. Vocabulary and grammar tests are typical measures of this ability. Reading comprehension or paragraph interpretation questions are common in many kinds of civil service tests. You are given a paragraph of written material and asked to find its central meaning.

3) Numerical ability

Number skills can be tested by the familiar arithmetic problem, by checking paired lists of numbers to see which are alike and which are different, or by interpreting charts and graphs. In the latter test, a graph may be printed in the test booklet which you are asked to use as the basis for answering questions.

4) Observation

A popular test for law-enforcement positions is the observation test. A picture is shown to you for several minutes, then taken away. Questions about the picture test your ability to observe both details and larger elements.

5) Following directions

In many positions in the public service, the employee must be able to carry out written instructions dependably and accurately. You may be given a chart with several columns, each column listing a variety of information. The questions require you to carry out directions involving the information given in the chart.

6) Skills and aptitudes

Performance tests effectively measure some manual skills and aptitudes. When the skill is one in which you are trained, such as typing or shorthand, you can practice. These tests are often very much like those given in business school or high school courses. For many of the other skills and aptitudes, however, no short-time preparation can be made. Skills and abilities natural to you or that you have developed throughout your lifetime are being tested.

Many of the general questions just described provide all the data needed to answer the questions and ask you to use your reasoning ability to find the answers. Your best preparation for these tests, as well as for tests of facts and ideas, is to be at your physical and mental best. You, no doubt, have your own methods of getting into an exam-taking mood and keeping “in shape.” The next section lists some ideas on this subject.

IV. KINDS OF QUESTIONS

Only rarely is the “essay” question, which you answer in narrative form, used in civil service tests. Civil service tests are usually of the short-answer type. Full instructions for answering these questions will be given to you at the examination. But in case this is your first experience with short-answer questions and separate answer sheets, here is what you need to know:

1) Multiple-choice Questions

Most popular of the short-answer questions is the "multiple choice" or "best answer" question. It can be used, for example, to test for factual knowledge, ability to solve problems or judgment in meeting situations found at work.

A multiple-choice question is normally one of three types—

- It can begin with an incomplete statement followed by several possible endings. You are to find the one ending which *best* completes the statement, although some of the others may not be entirely wrong.
- It can also be a complete statement in the form of a question which is answered by choosing one of the statements listed.
- It can be in the form of a problem – again you select the best answer.

Here is an example of a multiple-choice question with a discussion which should give you some clues as to the method for choosing the right answer:

When an employee has a complaint about his assignment, the action which will *best* help him overcome his difficulty is to

A. discuss his difficulty with his coworkers
B. take the problem to the head of the organization
C. take the problem to the person who gave him the assignment
D. say nothing to anyone about his complaint

In answering this question, you should study each of the choices to find which is best. Consider choice "A" – Certainly an employee may discuss his complaint with fellow employees, but no change or improvement can result, and the complaint remains unresolved. Choice "B" is a poor choice since the head of the organization probably does not know what assignment you have been given, and taking your problem to him is known as "going over the head" of the supervisor. The supervisor, or person who made the assignment, is the person who can clarify it or correct any injustice. Choice "C" is, therefore, correct. To say nothing, as in choice "D," is unwise. Supervisors have and interest in knowing the problems employees are facing, and the employee is seeking a solution to his problem.

2) True/False Questions

The "true/false" or "right/wrong" form of question is sometimes used. Here a complete statement is given. Your job is to decide whether the statement is right or wrong.

SAMPLE: A roaming cell-phone call to a nearby city costs less than a non-roaming call to a distant city.

This statement is wrong, or false, since roaming calls are more expensive.

This is not a complete list of all possible question forms, although most of the others are variations of these common types. You will always get complete directions for answering questions. Be sure you understand *how* to mark your answers – ask questions until you do.

V. RECORDING YOUR ANSWERS

Computer terminals are used more and more today for many different kinds of exams.

For an examination with very few applicants, you may be told to record your answers in the test booklet itself. Separate answer sheets are much more common. If this separate answer sheet is to be scored by machine – and this is often the case – it is highly important that you mark your answers correctly in order to get credit.

An electronic scoring machine is often used in civil service offices because of the speed with which papers can be scored. Machine-scored answer sheets must be marked with a pencil, which will be given to you. This pencil has a high graphite content which responds to the electronic scoring machine. As a matter of fact, stray dots may register as answers, so do not let your pencil rest on the answer sheet while you are pondering the correct answer. Also, if your pencil lead breaks or is otherwise defective, ask for another.

Since the answer sheet will be dropped in a slot in the scoring machine, be careful not to bend the corners or get the paper crumpled.

The answer sheet normally has five vertical columns of numbers, with 30 numbers to a column. These numbers correspond to the question numbers in your test booklet. After each number, going across the page are four or five pairs of dotted lines. These short dotted lines have small letters or numbers above them. The first two pairs may also have a "T" or "F" above the letters. This indicates that the first two pairs only are to be used if the questions are of the true-false type. If the questions are multiple choice, disregard the "T" and "F" and pay attention only to the small letters or numbers.

Answer your questions in the manner of the sample that follows:

32. The largest city in the United States is
    - A. Washington, D.C.
    - B. New York City
    - C. Chicago
    - D. Detroit
    - E. San Francisco

1) Choose the answer you think is best. (New York City is the largest, so "B" is correct.)
2) Find the row of dotted lines numbered the same as the question you are answering. (Find row number 32)
3) Find the pair of dotted lines corresponding to the answer. (Find the pair of lines under the mark "B.")
4) Make a solid black mark between the dotted lines.

VI. BEFORE THE TEST

Common sense will help you find procedures to follow to get ready for an examination. Too many of us, however, overlook these sensible measures. Indeed, nervousness and fatigue have been found to be the most serious reasons why applicants fail to do their best on civil service tests. Here is a list of reminders:

- Begin your preparation early – Don't wait until the last minute to go scurrying around for books and materials or to find out what the position is all about.
- Prepare continuously – An hour a night for a week is better than an all-night cram session. This has been definitely established. What is more, a night a week for a month will return better dividends than crowding your study into a shorter period of time.
- Locate the place of the exam – You have been sent a notice telling you when and where to report for the examination. If the location is in a different town or otherwise unfamiliar to you, it would be well to inquire the best route and learn something about the building.
- Relax the night before the test – Allow your mind to rest. Do not study at all that night. Plan some mild recreation or diversion; then go to bed early and get a good night's sleep.
- Get up early enough to make a leisurely trip to the place for the test – This way unforeseen events, traffic snarls, unfamiliar buildings, etc. will not upset you.
- Dress comfortably – A written test is not a fashion show. You will be known by number and not by name, so wear something comfortable.
- Leave excess paraphernalia at home – Shopping bags and odd bundles will get in your way. You need bring only the items mentioned in the official notice you received; usually everything you need is provided. Do not bring reference books to the exam. They will only confuse those last minutes and be taken away from you when in the test room.
- Arrive somewhat ahead of time – If because of transportation schedules you must get there very early, bring a newspaper or magazine to take your mind off yourself while waiting.
- Locate the examination room – When you have found the proper room, you will be directed to the seat or part of the room where you will sit. Sometimes you are given a sheet of instructions to read while you are waiting. Do not fill out any forms until you are told to do so; just read them and be prepared.
- Relax and prepare to listen to the instructions
- If you have any physical problem that may keep you from doing your best, be sure to tell the test administrator. If you are sick or in poor health, you really cannot do your best on the exam. You can come back and take the test some other time.

VII. AT THE TEST

The day of the test is here and you have the test booklet in your hand. The temptation to get going is very strong. Caution! There is more to success than knowing the right answers. You must know how to identify your papers and understand variations in the type of short-answer question used in this particular examination. Follow these suggestions for maximum results from your efforts:

1) Cooperate with the monitor

The test administrator has a duty to create a situation in which you can be as much at ease as possible. He will give instructions, tell you when to begin, check to see that you are marking your answer sheet correctly, and so on. He is not there to guard you, although he will see that your competitors do not take unfair advantage. He wants to help you do your best.

2) Listen to all instructions

Don't jump the gun! Wait until you understand all directions. In most civil service tests you get more time than you need to answer the questions. So don't be in a hurry. Read each word of instructions until you clearly understand the meaning. Study the examples, listen to all announcements and follow directions. Ask questions if you do not understand what to do.

3) Identify your papers

Civil service exams are usually identified by number only. You will be assigned a number; you must not put your name on your test papers. Be sure to copy your number correctly. Since more than one exam may be given, copy your exact examination title.

4) Plan your time

Unless you are told that a test is a "speed" or "rate of work" test, speed itself is usually not important. Time enough to answer all the questions will be provided, but this does not mean that you have all day. An overall time limit has been set. Divide the total time (in minutes) by the number of questions to determine the approximate time you have for each question.

5) Do not linger over difficult questions

If you come across a difficult question, mark it with a paper clip (useful to have along) and come back to it when you have been through the booklet. One caution if you do this – be sure to skip a number on your answer sheet as well. Check often to be sure that you have not lost your place and that you are marking in the row numbered the same as the question you are answering.

6) Read the questions

Be sure you know what the question asks! Many capable people are unsuccessful because they failed to *read* the questions correctly.

7) Answer all questions

Unless you have been instructed that a penalty will be deducted for incorrect answers, it is better to guess than to omit a question.

8) Speed tests

It is often better NOT to guess on speed tests. It has been found that on timed tests people are tempted to spend the last few seconds before time is called in marking answers at random – without even reading them – in the hope of picking up a few extra points. To discourage this practice, the instructions may warn you that your score will be "corrected" for guessing. That is, a penalty will be applied. The incorrect answers will be deducted from the correct ones, or some other penalty formula will be used.

9) Review your answers

If you finish before time is called, go back to the questions you guessed or omitted to give them further thought. Review other answers if you have time.

10) Return your test materials

If you are ready to leave before others have finished or time is called, take ALL your materials to the monitor and leave quietly. Never take any test material with you. The monitor can discover whose papers are not complete, and taking a test booklet may be grounds for disqualification.

VIII. EXAMINATION TECHNIQUES

1) Read the general instructions carefully. These are usually printed on the first page of the exam booklet. As a rule, these instructions refer to the timing of the examination; the fact that you should not start work until the signal and must stop work at a signal, etc. If there are any *special* instructions, such as a choice of questions to be answered, make sure that you note this instruction carefully.

2) When you are ready to start work on the examination, that is as soon as the signal has been given, read the instructions to each question booklet, underline any key words or phrases, such as *least*, *best*, *outline*, *describe* and the like. In this way you will tend to answer as requested rather than discover on reviewing your paper that you *listed without describing*, that you selected the *worst* choice rather than the *best* choice, etc.

3) If the examination is of the objective or multiple-choice type – that is, each question will also give a series of possible answers: A, B, C or D, and you are called upon to select the best answer and write the letter next to that answer on your answer paper – it is advisable to start answering each question in turn. There may be anywhere from 50 to 100 such questions in the three or four hours allotted and you can see how much time would be taken if you read through all the questions before beginning to answer any. Furthermore, if you come across a question or group of questions which you know would be difficult to answer, it would undoubtedly affect your handling of all the other questions.

4) If the examination is of the essay type and contains but a few questions, it is a moot point as to whether you should read all the questions before starting to answer any one. Of course, if you are given a choice – say five out of seven and the like – then it is essential to read all the questions so you can eliminate the two that are most difficult. If, however, you are asked to answer all the questions, there may be danger in trying to answer the easiest one first because you may find that you will spend too much time on it. The best technique is to answer the first question, then proceed to the second, etc.

5) Time your answers. Before the exam begins, write down the time it started, then add the time allowed for the examination and write down the time it must be completed, then divide the time available somewhat as follows:

- If 3-1/2 hours are allowed, that would be 210 minutes. If you have 80 objective-type questions, that would be an average of 2-1/2 minutes per question. Allow yourself no more than 2 minutes per question, or a total of 160 minutes, which will permit about 50 minutes to review.
- If for the time allotment of 210 minutes there are 7 essay questions to answer, that would average about 30 minutes a question. Give yourself only 25 minutes per question so that you have about 35 minutes to review.

6) The most important instruction is to *read each question* and make sure you know what is wanted. The second most important instruction is to *time yourself properly* so that you answer every question. The third most important instruction is to *answer every question*. Guess if you have to but include something for each question. Remember that you will receive no credit for a blank and will probably receive some credit if you write something in answer to an essay question. If you guess a letter – say "B" for a multiple-choice question – you may have guessed right. If you leave a blank as an answer to a multiple-choice question, the examiners may respect your feelings but it will not add a point to your score. Some exams may penalize you for wrong answers, so in such cases *only*, you may not want to guess unless you have some basis for your answer.

7) Suggestions
   a. Objective-type questions
      1. Examine the question booklet for proper sequence of pages and questions
      2. Read all instructions carefully
      3. Skip any question which seems too difficult; return to it after all other questions have been answered
      4. Apportion your time properly; do not spend too much time on any single question or group of questions
      5. Note and underline key words – *all, most, fewest, least, best, worst, same, opposite,* etc.
      6. Pay particular attention to negatives
      7. Note unusual option, e.g., unduly long, short, complex, different or similar in content to the body of the question
      8. Observe the use of "hedging" words – *probably, may, most likely,* etc.
      9. Make sure that your answer is put next to the same number as the question
      10. Do not second-guess unless you have good reason to believe the second answer is definitely more correct
      11. Cross out original answer if you decide another answer is more accurate; do not erase until you are ready to hand your paper in
      12. Answer all questions; guess unless instructed otherwise
      13. Leave time for review

   b. Essay questions
      1. Read each question carefully
      2. Determine exactly what is wanted. Underline key words or phrases.
      3. Decide on outline or paragraph answer

4. Include many different points and elements unless asked to develop any one or two points or elements
5. Show impartiality by giving pros and cons unless directed to select one side only
6. Make and write down any assumptions you find necessary to answer the questions
7. Watch your English, grammar, punctuation and choice of words
8. Time your answers; don't crowd material

8) Answering the essay question

Most essay questions can be answered by framing the specific response around several key words or ideas. Here are a few such key words or ideas:

M's: manpower, materials, methods, money, management
P's: purpose, program, policy, plan, procedure, practice, problems, pitfalls, personnel, public relations

a. Six basic steps in handling problems:
    1. Preliminary plan and background development
    2. Collect information, data and facts
    3. Analyze and interpret information, data and facts
    4. Analyze and develop solutions as well as make recommendations
    5. Prepare report and sell recommendations
    6. Install recommendations and follow up effectiveness

b. Pitfalls to avoid
    1. *Taking things for granted* – A statement of the situation does not necessarily imply that each of the elements is necessarily true; for example, a complaint may be invalid and biased so that all that can be taken for granted is that a complaint has been registered
    2. *Considering only one side of a situation* – Wherever possible, indicate several alternatives and then point out the reasons you selected the best one
    3. *Failing to indicate follow up* – Whenever your answer indicates action on your part, make certain that you will take proper follow-up action to see how successful your recommendations, procedures or actions turn out to be
    4. *Taking too long in answering any single question* – Remember to time your answers properly

IX. AFTER THE TEST

Scoring procedures differ in detail among civil service jurisdictions although the general principles are the same. Whether the papers are hand-scored or graded by machine we have described, they are nearly always graded by number. That is, the person who marks the paper knows only the number – never the name – of the applicant. Not until all the papers have been graded will they be matched with names. If other tests, such as training and experience or oral interview ratings have been given, scores will be combined. Different parts of the examination usually have different weights. For example, the written test might count 60 percent of the final grade, and a rating of training and experience 40 percent. In many jurisdictions, veterans will have a certain number of points added to their grades.

After the final grade has been determined, the names are placed in grade order and an eligible list is established. There are various methods for resolving ties between those who get the same final grade – probably the most common is to place first the name of the person whose application was received first. Job offers are made from the eligible list in the order the names appear on it. You will be notified of your grade and your rank as soon as all these computations have been made. This will be done as rapidly as possible.

People who are found to meet the requirements in the announcement are called "eligibles." Their names are put on a list of eligible candidates. An eligible's chances of getting a job depend on how high he stands on this list and how fast agencies are filling jobs from the list.

When a job is to be filled from a list of eligibles, the agency asks for the names of people on the list of eligibles for that job. When the civil service commission receives this request, it sends to the agency the names of the three people highest on this list. Or, if the job to be filled has specialized requirements, the office sends the agency the names of the top three persons who meet these requirements from the general list.

The appointing officer makes a choice from among the three people whose names were sent to him. If the selected person accepts the appointment, the names of the others are put back on the list to be considered for future openings.

That is the rule in hiring from all kinds of eligible lists, whether they are for typist, carpenter, chemist, or something else. For every vacancy, the appointing officer has his choice of any one of the top three eligibles on the list. This explains why the person whose name is on top of the list sometimes does not get an appointment when some of the persons lower on the list do. If the appointing officer chooses the second or third eligible, the No. 1 eligible does not get a job at once, but stays on the list until he is appointed or the list is terminated.

X. HOW TO PASS THE INTERVIEW TEST

The examination for which you applied requires an oral interview test. You have already taken the written test and you are now being called for the interview test – the final part of the formal examination.

You may think that it is not possible to prepare for an interview test and that there are no procedures to follow during an interview. Our purpose is to point out some things you can do in advance that will help you and some good rules to follow and pitfalls to avoid while you are being interviewed.

What is an interview supposed to test?

The written examination is designed to test the technical knowledge and competence of the candidate; the oral is designed to evaluate intangible qualities, not readily measured otherwise, and to establish a list showing the relative fitness of each candidate – as measured against his competitors – for the position sought. Scoring is not on the basis of "right" and "wrong," but on a sliding scale of values ranging from "not passable" to "outstanding." As a matter of fact, it is possible to achieve a relatively low score without a single "incorrect" answer because of evident weakness in the qualities being measured.

Santa Clara County Library District

408-293-2326

Checked Out Items 3/13/2020 17:57

XXXXXXXXXX8264

Item Title	Due Date
1. Principal administrative analyst : test preparation study guide : questions _ answers. 33305242618019	4/24/2020
2. CISA exam secrets study guide : your key to exam success : CISA test review for the certified information systems auditor exam. 33305239851961	4/24/2020

No of Items: 2

Amount Outstanding: $5.75

24/7 Telecirc: 800-471-0991

www.sccl.org

Thank you for visiting our library.

Occasionally, an examination may consist entirely of an oral test – either an individual or a group oral. In such cases, information is sought concerning the technical knowledges and abilities of the candidate, since there has been no written examination for this purpose. More commonly, however, an oral test is used to supplement a written examination.

Who conducts interviews?

The composition of oral boards varies among different jurisdictions. In nearly all, a representative of the personnel department serves as chairman. One of the members of the board may be a representative of the department in which the candidate would work. In some cases, "outside experts" are used, and, frequently, a businessman or some other representative of the general public is asked to serve. Labor and management or other special groups may be represented. The aim is to secure the services of experts in the appropriate field.

However the board is composed, it is a good idea (and not at all improper or unethical) to ascertain in advance of the interview who the members are and what groups they represent. When you are introduced to them, you will have some idea of their backgrounds and interests, and at least you will not stutter and stammer over their names.

What should be done before the interview?

While knowledge about the board members is useful and takes some of the surprise element out of the interview, there is other preparation which is more substantive. It *is* possible to prepare for an oral interview – in several ways:

1) Keep a copy of your application and review it carefully before the interview

This may be the only document before the oral board, and the starting point of the interview. Know what education and experience you have listed there, and the sequence and dates of all of it. Sometimes the board will ask you to review the highlights of your experience for them; you should not have to hem and haw doing it.

2) Study the class specification and the examination announcement

Usually, the oral board has one or both of these to guide them. The qualities, characteristics or knowledges required by the position sought are stated in these documents. They offer valuable clues as to the nature of the oral interview. For example, if the job involves supervisory responsibilities, the announcement will usually indicate that knowledge of modern supervisory methods and the qualifications of the candidate as a supervisor will be tested. If so, you can expect such questions, frequently in the form of a hypothetical situation which you are expected to solve. NEVER go into an oral without knowledge of the duties and responsibilities of the job you seek.

3) Think through each qualification required

Try to visualize the kind of questions you would ask if you were a board member. How well could you answer them? Try especially to appraise your own knowledge and background in each area, *measured against the job sought*, and identify any areas in which you are weak. Be critical and realistic – do not flatter yourself.

4) Do some general reading in areas in which you feel you may be weak

For example, if the job involves supervision and your past experience has NOT, some general reading in supervisory methods and practices, particularly in the field of human relations, might be useful. Do NOT study agency procedures or detailed manuals. The oral board will be testing your understanding and capacity, not your memory.

5) Get a good night's sleep and watch your general health and mental attitude

You will want a clear head at the interview. Take care of a cold or any other minor ailment, and of course, no hangovers.

What should be done on the day of the interview?

Now comes the day of the interview itself. Give yourself plenty of time to get there. Plan to arrive somewhat ahead of the scheduled time, particularly if your appointment is in the fore part of the day. If a previous candidate fails to appear, the board might be ready for you a bit early. By early afternoon an oral board is almost invariably behind schedule if there are many candidates, and you may have to wait. Take along a book or magazine to read, or your application to review, but leave any extraneous material in the waiting room when you go in for your interview. In any event, relax and compose yourself.

The matter of dress is important. The board is forming impressions about you – from your experience, your manners, your attitude, and your appearance. Give your personal appearance careful attention. Dress your best, but not your flashiest. Choose conservative, appropriate clothing, and be sure it is immaculate. This is a business interview, and your appearance should indicate that you regard it as such. Besides, being well groomed and properly dressed will help boost your confidence.

Sooner or later, someone will call your name and escort you into the interview room. *This is it.* From here on you are on your own. It is too late for any more preparation. But remember, you asked for this opportunity to prove your fitness, and you are here because your request was granted.

What happens when you go in?

The usual sequence of events will be as follows: The clerk (who is often the board stenographer) will introduce you to the chairman of the oral board, who will introduce you to the other members of the board. Acknowledge the introductions before you sit down. Do not be surprised if you find a microphone facing you or a stenotypist sitting by. Oral interviews are usually recorded in the event of an appeal or other review.

Usually the chairman of the board will open the interview by reviewing the highlights of your education and work experience from your application – primarily for the benefit of the other members of the board, as well as to get the material into the record. Do not interrupt or comment unless there is an error or significant misinterpretation; if that is the case, do not hesitate. But do not quibble about insignificant matters. Also, he will usually ask you some question about your education, experience or your present job – partly to get you to start talking and to establish the interviewing "rapport." He may start the actual questioning, or turn it over to one of the other members. Frequently, each member undertakes the questioning on a particular area, one in which he is perhaps most competent, so you can expect each member to participate in the examination. Because time is limited, you may also expect some rather abrupt switches in the direction the questioning takes, so do not be upset by it. Normally, a board member will not pursue a single line of questioning unless he discovers a particular strength or weakness.

After each member has participated, the chairman will usually ask whether any member has any further questions, then will ask you if you have anything you wish to add. Unless you are expecting this question, it may floor you. Worse, it may start you off on an extended, extemporaneous speech. The board is not usually seeking more information. The question is principally to offer you a last opportunity to present further qualifications or to indicate that you have nothing to add. So, if you feel that a significant qualification or characteristic has been overlooked, it is proper to point it out in a sentence or so. Do not compliment the board on the thoroughness of their examination – they have been sketchy, and you know it. If you wish, merely say, "No thank you, I have nothing further to add." This is a point where you can "talk yourself out" of a good impression or fail to present an important bit of information. Remember, *you close the interview yourself.*

The chairman will then say, "That is all, Mr. _______, thank you." Do not be startled; the interview is over, and quicker than you think. Thank him, gather your belongings and take your leave. Save your sigh of relief for the other side of the door.

How to put your best foot forward

Throughout this entire process, you may feel that the board individually and collectively is trying to pierce your defenses, seek out your hidden weaknesses and embarrass and confuse you. Actually, this is not true. They are obliged to make an appraisal of your qualifications for the job you are seeking, and they want to see you in your best light. Remember, they must interview all candidates and a non-cooperative candidate may become a failure in spite of their best efforts to bring out his qualifications. Here are 15 suggestions that will help you:

1) Be natural – Keep your attitude confident, not cocky

If you are not confident that you can do the job, do not expect the board to be. Do not apologize for your weaknesses, try to bring out your strong points. The board is interested in a positive, not negative, presentation. Cockiness will antagonize any board member and make him wonder if you are covering up a weakness by a false show of strength.

2) Get comfortable, but don't lounge or sprawl

Sit erectly but not stiffly. A careless posture may lead the board to conclude that you are careless in other things, or at least that you are not impressed by the importance of the occasion. Either conclusion is natural, even if incorrect. Do not fuss with your clothing, a pencil or an ashtray. Your hands may occasionally be useful to emphasize a point; do not let them become a point of distraction.

3) Do not wisecrack or make small talk

This is a serious situation, and your attitude should show that you consider it as such. Further, the time of the board is limited – they do not want to waste it, and neither should you.

4) Do not exaggerate your experience or abilities

In the first place, from information in the application or other interviews and sources, the board may know more about you than you think. Secondly, you probably will not get away with it. An experienced board is rather adept at spotting such a situation, so do not take the chance.

5) If you know a board member, do not make a point of it, yet do not hide it

Certainly you are not fooling him, and probably not the other members of the board. Do not try to take advantage of your acquaintanceship – it will probably do you little good.

6) Do not dominate the interview

Let the board do that. They will give you the clues – do not assume that you have to do all the talking. Realize that the board has a number of questions to ask you, and do not try to take up all the interview time by showing off your extensive knowledge of the answer to the first one.

7) Be attentive

You only have 20 minutes or so, and you should keep your attention at its sharpest throughout. When a member is addressing a problem or question to you, give him your undivided attention. Address your reply principally to him, but do not exclude the other board members.

8) Do not interrupt

A board member may be stating a problem for you to analyze. He will ask you a question when the time comes. Let him state the problem, and wait for the question.

9) Make sure you understand the question

Do not try to answer until you are sure what the question is. If it is not clear, restate it in your own words or ask the board member to clarify it for you. However, do not haggle about minor elements.

10) Reply promptly but not hastily

A common entry on oral board rating sheets is "candidate responded readily," or "candidate hesitated in replies." Respond as promptly and quickly as you can, but do not jump to a hasty, ill-considered answer.

11) Do not be peremptory in your answers

A brief answer is proper – but do not fire your answer back. That is a losing game from your point of view. The board member can probably ask questions much faster than you can answer them.

12) Do not try to create the answer you think the board member wants

He is interested in what kind of mind you have and how it works – not in playing games. Furthermore, he can usually spot this practice and will actually grade you down on it.

13) Do not switch sides in your reply merely to agree with a board member

Frequently, a member will take a contrary position merely to draw you out and to see if you are willing and able to defend your point of view. Do not start a debate, yet do not surrender a good position. If a position is worth taking, it is worth defending.

14) Do not be afraid to admit an error in judgment if you are shown to be wrong

The board knows that you are forced to reply without any opportunity for careful consideration. Your answer may be demonstrably wrong. If so, admit it and get on with the interview.

15) Do not dwell at length on your present job

The opening question may relate to your present assignment. Answer the question but do not go into an extended discussion. You are being examined for a *new* job, not your present one. As a matter of fact, try to phrase ALL your answers in terms of the job for which you are being examined.

Basis of Rating

Probably you will forget most of these “do’s” and “don’ts” when you walk into the oral interview room. Even remembering them all will not ensure you a passing grade. Perhaps you did not have the qualifications in the first place. But remembering them will help you to put your best foot forward, without treading on the toes of the board members.

Rumor and popular opinion to the contrary notwithstanding, an oral board wants you to make the best appearance possible. They know you are under pressure – but they also want to see how you respond to it as a guide to what your reaction would be under the pressures of the job you seek. They will be influenced by the degree of poise you display, the personal traits you show and the manner in which you respond.

ABOUT THIS BOOK

This book contains tests divided into Examination Sections. Go through each test, answering every question in the margin. At the end of each test look at the answer key and check your answers. On the ones you got wrong, look at the right answer choice and learn. Do not fill in the answers first. Do not memorize the questions and answers, but understand the answer and principles involved. On your test, the questions will likely be different from the samples. Questions are changed and new ones added. If you understand these past questions you should have success with any changes that arise. Tests may consist of several types of questions. We have additional books on each subject should more study be advisable or necessary for you. Finally, the more you study, the better prepared you will be. This book is intended to be the last thing you study before you walk into the examination room. Prior study of relevant texts is also recommended. NLC publishes some of these in our Fundamental Series. Knowledge and good sense are important factors in passing your exam. Good luck also helps. So now study this Passbook, absorb the material contained within and take that knowledge into the examination. Then do your best to pass that exam.

EXAMINATION SECTION

EXAMINATION SECTION
TEST 1

DIRECTIONS: Each question or incomplete statement is followed by several suggested answers or completions. Select the one that BEST answers the question or completes the statement. *PRINT THE LETTER OF THE CORRECT ANSWER IN THE SPACE AT THE RIGHT.*

1. Assume that a manager is preparing a list of reasons to justify making a major change in methods and procedures in his agency. 1.____
   Which of the following reasons would be LEAST appropriate on such a list?

   A. Improve the means for satisfying needs and wants of agency personnel
   B. Increase efficiency
   C. Intensify competition and stimulate loyalty to separate work groups
   D. Contribute to the individual and group satisfaction of agency personnel

2. Many managers recognize the benefits of decentralization but are concerned about the danger of over-relaxation of control as a result of increased delegation. 2.____
   Of the following, the MOST appropriate means of establishing proper control under decentralization is for the manager to

   A. establish detailed standards for all phases of operation
   B. shift his attention from operating details to appraisal of results
   C. keep himself informed by decreasing the time span covered by reports
   D. make unilateral decisions on difficult situations that arise in decentralized locations

3. In some agencies, the counsel to the agency head is given the right to bypass the chain of command and issue orders directly to the staff concerning matters that involve certain specific processes and practices. 3.____
   This situation MOST NEARLY illustrates the principle of

   A. the acceptance theory of authority
   B. multiple-linear authority
   C. splintered authority
   D. functional authority

4. Assume that a manager is writing a brief report to his superior outlining the advantages of matrix organization. Of the following, it would be INCORRECT to state that 4.____

   A. in matrix organization, a project is emphasized by designating one individual as the focal point for all matters pertaining to it
   B. utilization of manpower can be flexible in matrix organization because a reservoir of specialists is maintained in the line operations
   C. the usual line staff arrangement is generally reversed in matrix organization
   D. in matrix organization, responsiveness to project needs is generally faster due to establishing needed communication lines and decision points

5. It is commonly understood that communication is an important part of the administrative process. Which of the following is NOT a valid principle of the communication process in administration? 5.____

   A. The channels of communication should be spontaneous.
   B. The lines of communication should be as direct and as short as possible.
   C. Communications should be authenticated.
   D. The persons serving in communications centers should be competent.

6. The PRIMARY purpose of the quantitative approach in management is to 6.____

   A. identify better alternatives for management decision-making
   B. substitute data for judgment
   C. match opinions to data
   D. match data to opinions

7. If an executive wants to make a strong case for running his agency as a flat type of structure, he should point out that the PRIMARY advantage of doing so is to 7.____

   A. provide less experience in decision-making for agency personnel
   B. facilitate frequent contact between each superior and his immediate subordinates
   C. improve communication and unify attitudes
   D. improve communication and diversify attitudes

8. In deciding how detailed his delegation of authority to a subordinate should be, a manager should follow the general principle that 8.____

   A. delegation of authority is more detailed at the top of the organizational structure
   B. detailed delegation of authority is associated with detailed work assignments
   C. delegation of authority should be in sufficient detail to prevent overlapping assignments
   D. detailed delegation of authority is associated with broad work assignments

9. In recent years, newer and more fluid types of organizational forms have been developed. One of these is a type of free-form organization. Another name for this type of organization is the 9.____

   A. project organization
   B. semimix organization
   C. naturalistic structure
   D. semipermanent structure

10. Which of the following is the MAJOR objective of operational or management systems audits? 10.____

   A. Determining the number of personnel needed
   B. Recommending opportunities for improving operating and management practices
   C. Detecting fraud
   D. Determining organization problems

11. Assume that a manager observes that conflict exists between his agency and another operating agency of government. 11.____
Which of the following statements is the LEAST probable cause of this conflict?

A. Incompatibility between the agencies' goals but similarity in their resource allocations
B. Compatibility between agencies' goals and resources
C. Status differences between agency personnel
D. Differences in perceptions of each other's policies

12. Of the following, a MAJOR purpose of brainstorming as a problem-solving technique is to 12.____

A. develop the ability to concentrate
B. encourage creative thinking
C. evaluate employees' ideas
D. develop critical ability

13. The one of the following requirements which is LEAST likely to accompany regular delegation of work from a manager to a subordinate is a(n) 13.____

A. need to review the organization's workload
B. indication of what work the subordinate is to do
C. need to grant authority to the subordinate
D. obligation for the subordinate who accepts the work to try to complete it

14. Of the following, the one factor which is generally considered LEAST essential to successful committee operation is 14.____

A. stating a clear definition of the authority and scope of the committee
B. selecting the committee chairman carefully
C. limiting the size of the committee to four persons
D. limiting the subject matter to that which can be handled in group discussion

15. In using the program evaluation and review technique, the *critical path* is the path that 15.____

A. requires the shortest time
B. requires the longest time
C. focuses most attention on social constraints
D. focuses most attention on repetitious jobs

16. Which one of the following is LEAST characteristic of the management-by-objectives approach? 16.____

A. The scope within which the employee may exercise decision-making is broadened
B. The employee starts with a self-appraisal of his performances, abilities, and potential
C. Emphasis is placed on activities performed; activities orientation is maximized
D. Each employee participates in determining his own objectives

17. The function of management which puts into effect the decisions, plans, and programs that have previously been worked out for achieving the goals of the group is MOST appropriately called 17.____

A. scheduling
B. classifying
C. budgeting
D. directing

18. In the establishment of a plan to improve office productive efficiency, which of the following guidelines is LEAST helpful in setting sound work standards? 18.____

A. Employees must accept the plan's objectives.
B. Current production averages must be promulgated as work standards for a group.
C. The work flow must generally be fairly constant.
D. The operation of the plan must be expressed in terms understandable to the worker.

19. The one of the following activities which, generally speaking, is of *relatively* MAJOR importance at the lower-management level and of *somewhat* LESSER importance at higher-management levels is 19.____

A. actuating
B. forecasting
C. organizing
D. planning

20. Three styles of leadership exist: democratic, authoritarian, and laissez-faire. Of the following work situations, the one in which a democratic approach would normally be the MOST effective is when the work is 20.____

A. routine and moderately complex
B. repetitious and simple
C. complex and not routine
D. simple and not routine

21. Governmental and business organizations *generally* encounter the GREATEST difficulties in developing tangible measures of which one of the following? 21.____

A. The level of expenditures
B. Contributions to social welfare
C. Retention rates
D. Causes of labor unrest

22. Of the following, a *management-by-objectives* program is BEST described as 22.____

A. a new comprehensive plan of organization
B. introduction of budgets and financial controls
C. introduction of long–range planning
D. development of future goals with supporting and related progress reviews

23. Research and analysis is probably the most widely used technique for selecting alternatives when major planning decisions are involved. 23.____
Of the following, a VALUABLE characteristic of research and analysis is that this technique

A. places the problem in a meaningful conceptual framework
B. involves practical application of the various alternatives
C. accurately analyzes all important tangibles
D. is much less expensive than other problem-solving methods

24. If a manager were assigned the task of using a systems approach to designing a new work unit, which of the following should he consider FIRST in carrying out his design? 24.____

A. Networks
B. Work flows and information processes
C. Linkages and relationships
D. Decision points and control loops

25. The MAIN distinction between Theory *X* and Theory *Y* approaches to organization, in accordance with Douglas McGregor's view, is that Theory *Y* 25.____

A. considers that work is natural to people; Theory *X* assumes that people are lazy and avoid work
B. leads to a tall, narrow organization structure, while Theory *X* leads to one that is flat
C. organizations motivate people with money; Theory *X* organizations motivate people with good working conditions
D. represents authoritarian management, while Theory *X* management is participative

---

KEY (CORRECT ANSWERS)

1. C
2. B
3. D
4. C
5. A
6. A
7. C
8. B
9. A
10. B
11. B
12. B
13. A
14. C
15. B
16. C
17. D
18. B
19. A
20. C
21. B
22. D
23. A
24. B
25. A

TEST 2

DIRECTIONS: Each question or incomplete statement is followed by several suggested answers or completions. Select the one that BEST answers the question or completes the statement. *PRINT THE LETTER OF THE CORRECT ANSWER IN THE SPACE AT THE RIGHT.*

1. Of the following, the stage in decision-making which is usually MOST difficult is 1.____

   A. stating the alternatives
   B. predicting the possible outcome of each alternative
   C. evaluating the relative merits of each alternative
   D. minimizing the undesirable aspects of the alternative selected

2. In a department where a clerk is reporting both to a senior clerk in charge of the mail room and also to a supervising clerk in charge of the duplicating section, there may be a breakdown of the management principle called 2.____

   A. horizontal specialization
   B. job enrichment
   C. unity of command
   D. Graicunas' Law

3. Of the following, the failure by line managers to accept and appreciate the benefits and limitations of a new program or system VERY frequently can be traced to the 3.____

   A. budgetary problems involved
   B. resultant need to reduce staff
   C. lack of controls it engenders
   D. failure of top management to support its implementation

4. Although there is general agreement that *management by objectives* has made a major contribution to modern management of large organizations, criticisms of the system during the past few years have resulted in 4.____

   A. mounting pressure for relaxation of management goals
   B. renewed concern with human values and the manager's personal needs
   C. over-mechanistic application of the perceptions of the behavioral scientists
   D. disillusionment with *management by objectives* on the part of a majority of managers

5. Of the following, which is usually considered to be a MAJOR obstacle to the systematic analysis of potential problems by managers? 5.____

   A. Managers have a tendency to think that all the implications of some proposed step cannot be fully understood.
   B. Rewards rarely go to those managers who are most successful at resolving current problems in management.
   C. There is a common conviction of managers that their goals are difficult to achieve.
   D. Managers are far more concerned about correcting today's problems than with preventing tomorrow's.

6. Which of the following should generally have the MOST influence on the selection of supervisors? 6.____

   A. Experience within the work unit where the vacancies exist
   B. Amount of money needed to effect the promotion
   C. Personal preferences of the administration
   D. Evaluation of capacity to exercise supervisory responsibilities

7. In questioning a potential administrator for selection purposes, the one of the following practices which is MOST desirable is to 7.____

   A. encourage the job applicant to give primarily *yes* or *no* replies
   B. get the applicant to talk freely and in detail about his background
   C. let the job applicant speak most of the time
   D. probe the applicant's attitudes, motivation, and willingness to accept responsibility

8. In implementing the managerial function of training subordinates, it is USEFUL to know that a widely agreed-upon definition of human learning is that learning 8.____

   A. is a relatively permanent change in behavior that results from reinforced practice or experience
   B. involves an improvement, but not necessarily a change in behavior
   C. involves a change in behavior, but not necessarily an improvement
   D. is a temporary change in behavior which must be subject to practice or experience

9. If a manager were thinking about using a committee of subordinates to solve an operating problem, which of the following would generally NOT be an advantage of such use of the committee approach? 9.____

   A. Improved coordination
   B. Low cost
   C. Increased motivation
   D. Integrated judgment

10. Which one of the following management approaches MOST often uses model-building techniques to solve management problems? 10.____
    _______ approach

   A. Behavioral
   B. Fiscal
   C. Quantitative
   D. Process

11. Of the following, the MOST serious risk in using budgets as a tool for management control is the 11.____

   A. probable neglect of other good management practices
   B. likelihood of guesswork because of the need to plan far in advance
   C. possibility of undue emphasis on factors that are easiest to measure
   D. danger of making qualitative rather than quantitative assessments of performance

12. In government budgeting, the problem of relating financial transactions to the fiscal year in which they are budgeted is BEST met by 12.____

    A. determining the cash balance by comparing how much money has been received and how much has been paid out
    B. applying net revenue to the fiscal year in which they are collected as offset by relevant expenses
    C. adopting a system whereby appropriations are entered when they are received and expenditures are entered when they are paid out
    D. entering expenditures on the books when the obligation to make the expenditure is made

13. If the agency's bookkeeping system records income when it is received and expenditures when the money is paid out, this sytem is USUALLY known as a ______ system. 13.____

    A. cash
    B. flow-payment
    C. deferred
    D. fiscal year income

14. An audit, as the term applies to budget execution, is MOST NEARLY a 14.____

    A. procedure based on the budget estimates
    B. control exercised by the executive on the legislature in the establishment of program priorities
    C. check on the legality of expenditures and is based on the appropriations act
    D. requirement which must be met before funds can be spent

15. In government budgeting, there is a procedure known as *allotment.* 15.____
    Of the following statements which relate to allotment, select the one that is MOST generally considered to be correct.
    Allotment

    A. increases the practice of budget units coming back to the legislative branch for supplemental appropriations
    B. is simply an example of red tape
    C. eliminates the requirement of timing of expenditures
    D. is designed to prevent waste

16. In government budgeting, the establishment of the schedules of allotments is MOST generally the responsibility of the 16.____

    A. budget unit and the legislature
    B. budget unit and the executive
    C. budget unit *only*
    D. executive and the legislature

17. Of the following statements relating to preparation of an organization's budget request, which is the MOST generally valid precaution? 17.____

   A. Give specific instructions on the format of budget requests and required supporting data
   B. Because of the complexity of preparing a budget request, avoid argumentation to support the requests
   C. Put requests in whatever format is desirable
   D. Consider that final approval will be given to initial estimates

18. Of the following statements which relate to the budget process in a well-organized government, select the one that is MOST NEARLY correct. 18.____

   A. The budget cycle is the step-by-step process which is repeated each and every fiscal year.
   B. Securing approval of the budget does not take place within the budget cycle.
   C. The development of a new budget and putting it into effect is a two-step process known as the budget cycle.
   D. The fiscal period, usually a fiscal year, has no relation to the budget cycle.

19. If a manager were asked what PPBS stands for, he would be RIGHT if he said 19.____

   A. public planning budgeting system
   B. planning programming budgeting system
   C. planning projections budgeting system
   D. programming procedures budgeting system

Questions 20–21.

DIRECTIONS: Answer Questions 20 and 21 on the basis of the following information.

<u>*Sample Budget*</u>

Refuse Collection	*Amount*
Personal Services	*$ 30,000*
Contractual Services	*5,000*
Supplies and Materials	*5,000*
Capital Outlay	*10,000*
	$ 50,000

Residential Collections		
Dwellings–1 pickup per week		*1,000*
Tons of refuse collected per year		*375*
Cost of collections per ton	*$*	*8*
Cost per dwelling pickup per year	*$*	*3*
Total annual cost	*$*	*3,000*

20. The sample budget shown is a simplified example of a ______ budget. 20.____

A. factorial
B. performance
C. qualitative
D. rational

21. The budget shown in the sample differs CHIEFLY from line-item and program budgets in that it includes 21.____

A. objects of expenditure but not activities or functions
B. only activities, functions, and control
C. activities and functions but not objects of expenditures
D. levels of service

Question 22.

DIRECTIONS: Answer Question 22 on the basis of the following information.

Sample Budget

Environmental Safety		
Air Pollution Protection		
Personal Services	*$20,000,000*	
Contractual Services	*4,000,000*	
Supplies and Materials	*4,000,000*	
Capital Outlay	*2,000,000*	
Total Air Pollution Protection		*$ 30,000,000*
Water Pollution Protection		
Personal Services	*$23,000,000*	
Supplies and Materials	*4,500,000*	
Capital Outlay	*20,500,000*	
Total Water Pollution Protection		*$ 48,000,000*
Total Environmental Safety		*$ 78,000,000*

22. Based on the above budget, which is the MOST valid statement? 22.____

A. Environmental Safety, Air Pollution Protection, and Water Pollution Protection could all be considered program elements.
B. The object listings included water pollution protection and capital outlay.
C. Examples of the program element listings in the above are personal services and supplies and materials.
D. Contractual Services and Environmental Safety were the program element listings.

23. Which of the following is NOT an advantage of a program budget over a line-item budget? 23.____
A program budget

A. allows us to set up priority lists in deciding what activities we will spend our money on
B. gives us more control over expenditures than a line-item budget
C. is more informative in that we know the broad purposes of spending money
D. enables us to see if one program is getting much less money than the others

24. If a manager were trying to explain the fundamental difference between traditional accounting theory and practice and the newer practice of managerial accounting, he would be MOST accurate if he said that 24.____

A. traditional accounting practice focused on providing information for persons outside organizations, while managerial accounting focuses on providing information for people inside organizations
B. traditional accounting practice focused on providing information for persons inside organizations while managerial accounting focuses on providing information for persons outside organizations
C. managerial accounting is exclusively concerned with historical facts while traditional accounting stresses future projections exclusively
D. traditional accounting practice is more budget-focused than managerial accounting

25. Which of the following formulas is used to determine the number of days required to process work? 25.____

A. $\frac{\text{Employees x Daily Output}}{\text{Volume}}$ = Days to Process Work

B. $\frac{\text{Volume x Daily Output}}{\text{Employees}}$ = Days to Process Work

C. $\frac{\text{Volume}}{\text{Employees x Daily Output}}$ = Days to Process Work

D. $\frac{\text{Employees x Volume}}{\text{Daily Output}}$ = Days to Process Work

KEY (CORRECT ANSWERS)

1. C
2. C
3. D
4. B
5. D

6. D
7. D
8. A
9. B
10. C

11. C
12. D
13. A
14. C
15. D

16. C
17. A
18. A
19. B
20. B

21. D
22. A
23. B
24. A
25. C

TEST 3

DIRECTIONS: Each question or incomplete statement is followed by several suggested answers or completions. Select the one that BEST answers the question or completes the statement. *PRINT THE LETTER OF THE CORRECT ANSWER IN THE SPACE AT THE RIGHT.*

1. Electronic data processing equipment can produce more information faster than can be generated by any other means. 1.____
In view of this, the MOST important problem faced by management at present is to

   A. keep computers fully occupied
   B. find enough computer personnel
   C. assimilate and properly evaluate the information
   D. obtain funds to establish appropriate information systems

2. A well-designed management information system ESSENTIALLY provides each executive and manager the information he needs for 2.____

   A. determining computer time requirements
   B. planning and measuring results
   C. drawing a new organization chart
   D. developing a new office layout

3. It is generally agreed that management policies should be periodically reappraised and restated in accordance with current conditions. 3.____
Of the following, the approach which would be MOST effective in determining whether a policy should be revised is to

   A. conduct interviews with staff members at all levels in order to ascertain the relationship between the policy and actual practice
   B. make proposed revisions in the policy and apply it to current problems
   C. make up hypothetical situations using both the old policy and a revised version in order to make comparisons
   D. call a meeting of top level staff in order to discuss ways of revising the policy

4. Every manager has many occasions to lead a conference or participate in a conference of some sort. 4.____
Of the following statements that pertain to conferences and conference leadership, which is generally considered to be MOST valid?

   A. Since World War II, the trend has been toward fewer shared decisions and more conferences.
   B. The most important part of a conference leader's job is to direct discussion.
   C. In providing opportunities for group interaction, management should avoid consideration of its past management philosophy.
   D. A good administrator cannot lead a good conference if he is a poor public speaker.

5. Of the following, it is usually LEAST desirable for a conference leader to 5.____

   A. turn the question to the person who asked it
   B. summarize proceedings periodically
   C. make a practice of not repeating questions
   D. ask a question without indicating who is to reply

6. The behavioral school of management thought bases its beliefs on certain assumptions. Which of the following is NOT a belief of this school of thought? 6.____

   A. People tend to seek and accept responsibility.
   B. Most people can be creative in solving problems.
   C. People prefer security above all else.
   D. Commitment is the most important factor in motivating people.

7. The one of the following objectives which would be LEAST appropriate as a major goal of research in the field of human resources management is to 7.____

   A. predict future conditions, events, and manpower needs
   B. evaluate established policies, programs, and practices
   C. evaluate proposed policies, programs, and practices
   D. identify deficient organizational units and apply suitable penalties

8. Of the following general interviewing methods or techniques, the one that is USUALLY considered to be effective in counseling, grievances, and appraisal interviews is the _______ interview. 8.____

   A. directed B. non-directed
   C. panel D. patterned

9. The ESSENTIAL first phase of decision-making is 9.____

   A. finding alternative solutions
   B. making a diagnosis of the problem
   C. selecting the plan to follow
   D. analyzing and comparing alternative solutions

10. Assume that, in a certain organization, a situation has developed in which there is little difference in status or authority between individuals. 10.____
Which of the following would be the MOST likely result with regard to communication in this organization?

   A. Both the accuracy and flow of communication will be improved.
   B. Both the accuracy and flow of communication will substantially decrease.
   C. Employees will seek more formal lines of communication.
   D. Neither the flow nor the accuracy of communication will be improved over the former hierarchical structure.

11. The main function of many agency administrative offices is *information management.* Information that is received by an administrative officer may be classified as active or passive, depending upon whether or not it requires the recipient to take some action. 11.____
Of the following, the item received which is clearly the MOST active information is

   A. an appointment of a new staff member
   B. a payment voucher for a new desk
   C. a press release concerning a past city event
   D. the minutes of a staff meeting

12. Which one of the following sets BEST describes the general order in which to teach an operation to a new employee? 12.____

A. Prepare, present, tryout, follow-up
B. Prepare, test, tryout, re-test
C. Present, test, tryout, follow-up
D. Test, present, follow-up, re-test

13. Of the following, public employees may be separated from public service 13.____

A. for the same reasons which are generally acceptable for discharging employees in private industry
B. only under the most trying circumstances
C. under procedures that are neither formalized nor subject to review
D. solely in extreme cases involving offenses of gravest character

14. Of the following, the one LEAST considered to be a communication barrier is 14.____

A. group feedback
B. charged words
C. selective perception
D. symbolic meanings

15. Of the following ways for a manager to handle his appointments, the BEST way, according to experts in administration, generally is to 15.____

A. schedule his own appointments and inform his secretary not to reserve his time without his approval
B. encourage everyone to make appointments through his secretary and tell her when he makes his own appointments
C. see no one who has not made a previous appointment
D. permit anyone to see him without an appointment

16. Assume that a manager decides to examine closely one of five units under his supervision to uncover problems common to all five. 16.____
His research technique is MOST closely related to the method called

A. experimentation
B. simulation
C. linear analysis
D. sampling

17. If one views the process of management as a dynamic process, which one of the following functions is NOT a legitimate part of that process? 17.____

A. Communication
B. Decision-making
C. Organizational slack
D. Motivation

18. Which of the following would be the BEST statement of a budget-oriented purpose for a government administrator? To 18.____

A. provide 200 hours of instruction in basic reading for 3500 adult illiterates at a cost of $1 million in the next fiscal year
B. inform the public of adult educational programs
C. facilitate the transfer to a city agency of certain functions of a federally-funded program which is being phased out
D. improve the reading skills of the adult citizens in the city

19. Modern management philosophy and practices are changing to accommodate the expectations and motivations of organization personnel. 19.____
Which of the following terms INCORRECTLY describes these newer managerial approaches?

A. Rational management
B. Participative management
C. Decentralization
D. Democratic supervision

20. Management studies support the hypothesis that, in spite of the tendency of employees to censor the information communicated to their supervisor, subordinates are MORE likely to communicate problem-oriented information upward when they have 20.____

A. a long period of service in the organization
B. a high degree of trust in the supervisor
C. a high educational level
D. low status on the organizational ladder

KEY (CORRECT ANSWERS)

1. C
2. B
3. A
4. B
5. A

6. C
7. D
8. B
9. B
10. D

11. A
12. A
13. A
14. A
15. B

16. D
17. C
18. A
19. A
20. B

EXAMINATION SECTION
TEST 1

DIRECTIONS Each question or incomplete statement is followed by several suggested answers or completions. Select the one that BEST answers the question or completes the statement. *PRINT THE LETTER OF THE CORRECT ANSWER IN THE SPACE AT THE RIGHT.*

1. Of the following, the BEST statement concerning the placement of *Conclusions and Recommendations* in a management report is: 1.____

   A. Recommendations should always be included in a report unless the report presents the results of an investigation
   B. If a report presents conclusions, it must present recommendations
   C. Every statement that is a conclusion should grow out of facts given elsewhere in the report
   D. Conclusions and recommendations should always conclude the report because they depend on its contents

2. Assume you are preparing a systematic analysis of your agency's pest control program and its effect on eliminating rodent infestation of premises in a specific region. 2.____
   To omit from your report important facts which you originally received from the person to whom you are reporting is GENERALLY considered to be

   A. *desirable;* anyone who is likely to read the report can consult his files for extra information
   B. *undesirable;* the report should include major facts that are obtained as a result of your efforts
   C. *desirable;* the person you are reporting to does not
   D. pass the report on to others who lack his own familiarity with the subject
   E. *undesirable;* the report should include all of the facts that are obtained as a result of your efforts

3. Of all the nonverbal devices used in report writing, tables are used most frequently to enable a reader to compare statistical information more easily. Hence, it is important that an analyst know when to use tables. 3.____
   Which one of the following statements that relate to tables is generally considered to be LEAST valid?

   A. A table from an outside source must be acknowledged by the report writer.
   B. A table should be placed far in advance of the point where it is referred to or discussed in the report.
   C. The notes applying to a table are placed at the bottom of the table, rather than at the bottom of the page on which the table is found.
   D. A table should indicate the major factors that effect the data it contains.

4. Assume that an analyst writes reports which contain more detail than might be needed to serve their purpose. 4.____
   Such a practice is GENERALLY considered to be

A. *desirable* ; this additional detail permits maximized machine utilization
B. *undesirable;* if specifications of reports are defined when they are first set up, loss of flexibility will follow
C. *desirable;* everything ought to be recorded so it will be there if it is ever needed
D. *undesirable;* recipients of these reports are likely to discredit them entirely

5. Assume that an analyst is gathering certain types of information which can be obtained only through interrogation of the clientele by means of a questionnaire. 5.____
Which one of the following statements that relate to construction of the questionnaire is the MOST valid?

A. Stress, whenever possible, the use of leading questions.
B. Avoid questions which touch on personal prejudice or pride.
C. Opinions, as much as facts, should be sought.
D. There is no psychological advantage for starting with a question of high interest value.

Questions 6-10.

DIRECTIONS: Questions 6 through 10 consist of sentences lettered A, B, C, and D. For each question, choose the sentence which is stylistically and grammatically MOST appropriate for a management report.

6. 6.____
A. For too long, the citizen has been forced to rely for his productivity information on the whims, impressions and uninformed opinion of public spokesmen.
B. For too long, the citizen has been forced to base his information about productivity on the whims, impressions and uninformed opinion of public spokesmen.
C. The citizen has been forced to base his information about productivity on the whims, impressions and uninformed opinion of public spokesmen for too long.
D. The citizen has been forced for too long to rely for his productivity information on the whims, impressions and uninformed opinion of public spokesmen.

7. 7.____
A. More competition means lower costs to the city, thereby helping to compensate for inflation.
B. More competition, helping to compensate for inflation, means lower costs to the city.
C. Inflation may be compensated for by more competition, which will reduce the city's costs.
D. The costs to the city will be lessened by more competition, helping to compensate for inflation.

8. 8.____
A. Some objectives depend on equal efforts from others, particularly private interests and the federal government; for example, technical advancement.
B. Some objectives, such as technical advancement, depend on equal efforts from others, particularly private interests and the federal government.
C. Some objectives depend on equal efforts from others, particularly private interests and the federal government, such as technical advancement.
D. Some objectives depend on equal efforts from others (technical advancement, for example); particularly private interests and the federal government.

9. A. It has always been the practice of this office toeffectuate recruitment of prospective employees from other departments. 9.____
   B. This office has always made a practice of recruiting prospective employees from other departments.
   C. Recruitment of prospective employees from other departments has always been a practice which has been implemented by this office.
   D. Implementation of the policy of recruitment of prospective employees from other departments has always been a practice of this office.

10. A. These employees are assigned to the level of work evidenced by their efforts and skills during the training period. 10.____
   B. The level of work to which these employees is assigned is decided upon on the basis of the efforts and skills evidenced by them during the period in which they were trained.
   C. Assignment of these employees is made on the basis of the level of work their efforts and skills during the training period has evidenced.
   D. These employees are assigned to a level of work their efforts and skills during the training period have evidenced.

11. To overcome the manual collation problem, forms are frequently padded. 11.____
Of the following statements which relate to this type of packaging, select the one that is MOST accurate.

   A. Typewritten forms which are prepared as padded forms are more efficient than all other packaging.
   B. Padded forms are best suited for handwritten forms.
   C. It is difficult for a printer to pad form copies of different colors.
   D. Registration problems increase when cut-sheet forms are padded.

12. Most forms are cut from a standard mill sheet of paper. 12.____
This is the size on which forms dealers base their prices. Since an agency is paying for a full-size sheet of paper, it is the responsibility of the analyst to design forms so that as many as possible may be cut from the sheet without waste.
Of the following sizes, select the one that will cut from a standard mill sheet with the GREATEST waste and should, therefore, be avoided if possible.

   A. 4" x 6"   B. 5" x 8"   C. 9" x 12"   D. 8 1/2" x 14"

13. Assume that you are assigned the task of reducing the time and costs involved in completing a form that is frequently used in your agency. After analyzing the matter, you decide to reduce the writing requirements of the form through the use of ballot boxes and preprinted data. 13.____
If exact copy-to-copy registration of this form is necessary, it is MOST advisable to

   A. vary the sizes of the ballot boxes
   B. stagger the ballot boxes
   C. place the ballot boxes as close together as possible
   D. have the ballot boxes follow the captions

14. To overcome problems that are involved in the use of cut-sheet and padded forms, specialty forms have been developed. Normally, these forms are commercially manufactured rather than produced in-plant. Before designing a form as a specialty form, however, you should be assured that certain factors are present. 14.____
Which one of the following factors deserves LEAST consideration?

A. The form is to be used in quantities of 5,000 or more annually.
B. The forms will be prepared on equipment using either a pinfeed device or pressure rollers for continuous feed-through.
C. Two or more copies of the form set must be held together for further processing subsequent to the initial distribution of the form set.
D. Copies of the form will be identical and no items of data will be selectively eliminated from one or more copies of the form.

15. Although a well-planned form should require little explanation as to its completion, there are many occasions when the analyst will find it necessary to include instructions on the form to assure that the person completing it does so correctly. 15.____
With respect to such instructions, it is usually considered to be LEAST appropriate to place them

A. in footnotes at the bottom of the form
B. following the spaces to be completed
C. directly under the form's title
D. on the front of the form

16. One of the basic data-arrangement methods used in forms design is the *on-line* method. When this method is used, captions appear on the same line as the space provided for entry of the variable data. 16.____
This arrangement is NOT recommended because it

A. forces the typist to make use of the typewriter's tab stops, thus increasing processing time
B. wastes horizontal space since the caption appears on the writing line
C. tends to make the variable data become more dominant than the captions
D. increases the form's processing time by requiring the typist to continually roll the platen back and forth to expose the caption

17. Before designing a form for his agency, the analyst should be aware of certain basic design standards. 17.____
Which one of the following statements relating to horizontal and vertical spacing requirements is *generally* considered to be the MOST acceptable in forms design?

A. If the form will be completed by typewriter, no more than four writing lines to the vertical inch should be allowed.
B. If the form will be completed by hand, allowance should not be made for the different sizes of individual handwriting.
C. If the form will be completed partly by hand and partly by typewriter, the analyst should provide the same vertical spacing as for typewriter completion
D. The form should be designed with proportional spacing for pica and elite type.

18. As an analyst, you may be required to conduct a functional analysis of your agency's forms. 18.____
Which one of the following statements pertaining to this type of analysis is *generally* considered to be MOST valid?

A. Except for extremely low-volume forms, all forms should be functionally analyzed.
B. To obtain maximum benefit from the analysis, functional re-analyses of all forms should be undertaken at least once every three to six months.
C. All existing forms should be functionally analyzed before reorder.
D. Only new forms should be functionally analyzed prior to being authorized for adoption.

19. The analyst must assure the users of a form that its construction provides for the most efficient method in terms of how data will be entered and processed subsequent to their initial entry. 19.____
While the simplest construction is the cut sheet, the GREATEST disadvantage of this type of construction is

A. the non-productive *makeready* time required if multiple copies of a form must be simultaneously prepared
B. the difficulty experienced by users in filling in the forms solely by mechanical means
C. its uneconomical cost of production
D. the restrictions of limitations placed on the utilization of a variety of substances which may be used in form composition

20. Assume you have designed a form which requires data to be entered on multiple copies simultaneously. A determination has not yet been made whether to order the form as interleaved-carbon form sets or as carbonless forms. 20.____
The advantage of using carbonless forms is that they

A. permit more readable copies to be made at a single writing
B. average about 30 percent lower in price than conventional interleaved-carbon form sets
C. provide greater security if the information entered on the form is classified
D. are not subject to accidental imaging

KEY (CORRECT ANSWERS)

1. C
2. B
3. B
4. D
5. B

6. B
7. A
8. B
9. B
10. A

11. B
12. C
13. B
14. D
15. A

16. B
17. C
18. C
19. A
20. C

TEST 2

DIRECTIONS: Each question or incomplete statement is followed by several suggested answers or completions. Select the one that BEST answers the question or completes the statement. *PRINT THE LETTER OF THE CORRECT ANSWER IN THE SPACE AT THE RIGHT.*

1. Many analysts lean toward the use of varying colors of paper in a multiple-part form set to indicate distribution. This usage is GENERALLY considered to be 1.____

   A. *desirable;* it is more effective than using white paper for all copies and imprinting the distribution in the margin of the copy
   B. *undesirable;* colored inks should be used instead to indicate distribution in a multi-part form set
   C. *desirable;* it will lead to lower costs of form production
   D. *undesirable;* it causes operational difficulties if the form is to be microfilmed or optically scanned

2. After a form has been reviewed and approved by the analyst, it should be given an identifying number. The following items pertain to the form number. 2.____
   Which item is MOST appropriately included as a portion of the form number?

   A. Revision date
   B. Order quantity
   C. Retention period
   D. Organization unit responsible for the form

Questions 3-8

DIRECTIONS: Questions 3 through 8 should be answered on the basis of the following information.

Assume that the figure at the top of the next page is a systems flowchart specifically prepared for the purchasing department of a large municipal agency. Some of the symbols in the flowchart are incorrectly used. The symbols are numbered.

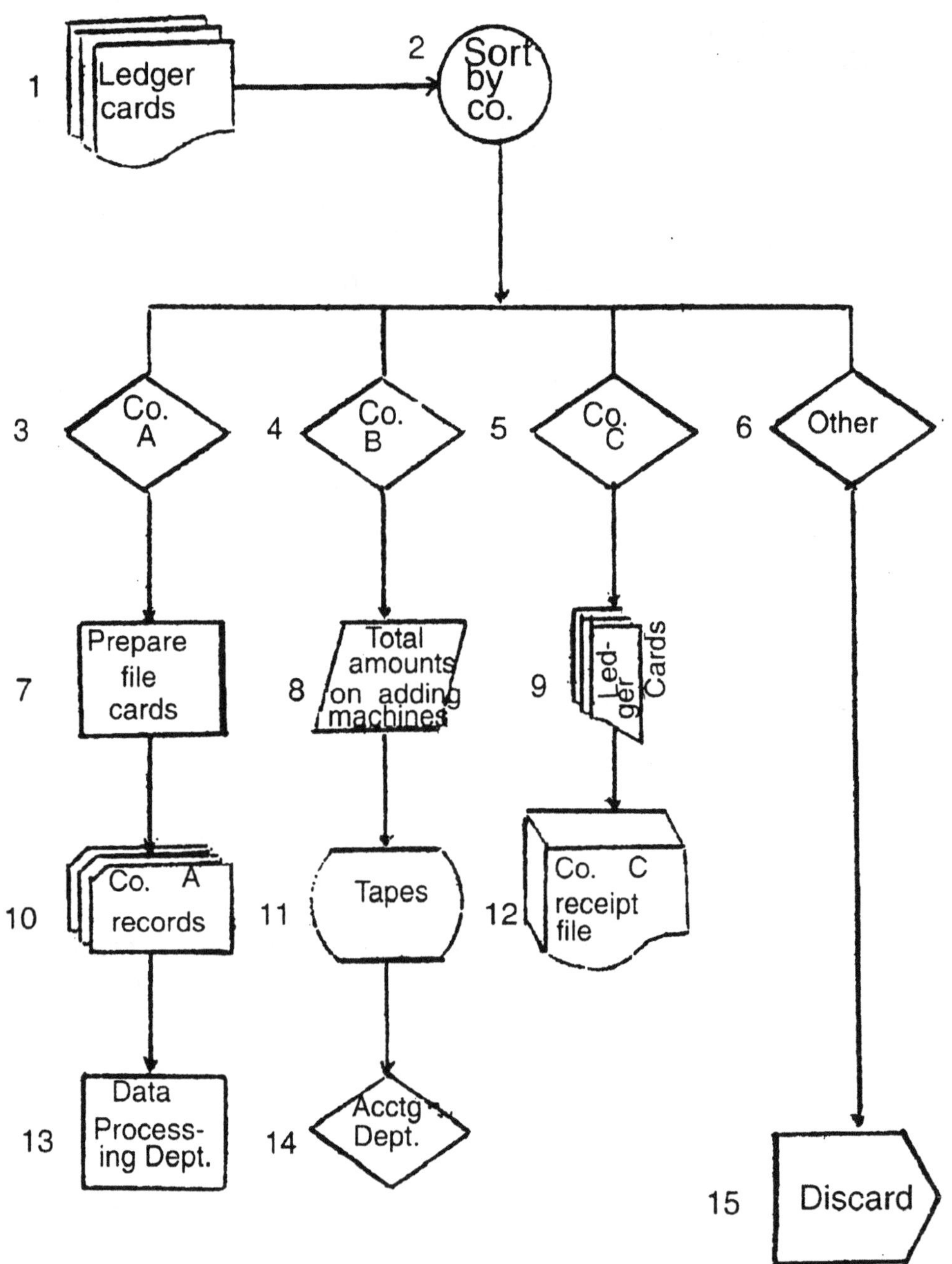

3. According to the flowchart, Number 2 is 3.____

   A. *correct*
   B. *incorrect;* the symbol should have six sides
   C. *incorrect;* the symbol should be the same as Number 7
   D. *incorrect;* the symbol should be the same as Number 8

4. According to the flowchart, Number 9 is 4.____

   A. *correct*
   B. *incorrect;* the symbol should be the same as Number 1

C. *incorrect;* the symbol should be the same as Number 7
D. *incorrect;* the symbol should be the same as Number 10

5. According to the flowchart, Number 11 is 5._____

A. *correct*
B. *incorrect;* the symbol should be the same as Number 13
C. *incorrect;* the symbol should be the same as Number 10
D. *incorrect;* the symbol should be the same as Number 9

6. According to the flowchart, Number 14 is 6._____

A. *correct*
B. *incorrect;* the symbol should have three sides
C. *incorrect;* the symbol should have six sides
D. *incorrect;* the symbol should have eight sides

7. According to the flowchart, Number 12 is 7._____

A. *correct*
B. *incorrect;* a *file* should be represented in the same form as the symbol which immediately precedes it
C. *incorrect;* the symbol should be the same as Number 13
D. *incorrect;* the symbol should be the same as Number 14

8. According to the flowchart, Number 15 is 8._____

A. *correct*
B. *incorrect;* the symbol should be 
C. *incorrect;* the symbol should be
D. *incorrect;* the symbol should be

9. An agency expects to increase its services, the workload of the office will increase, and additional equipment and personnel will probably be required. Although there is no set formula for determining how much space will be required in an agency in a specific number of years from now, certain guidelines have been developed to assist the analyst in dealing with the problem of providing expansion space. 9._____
Which of the following statements pertaining to this aspect of space utilization is *generally* considered to be the LEAST desirable practice?

A. Spread the departments to fit into space that is temporarily surplus and awaiting the day when it is needed
B. Place major departments where they can expand into the area of minor departments
C. Visualize the direction in which the expansion will go and avoid placing the relatively fixed installations in the way
D. Lay out the departments economically and screen off the surplus areas, using them for storage or other temporary usage

Questions 10-11.

DIRECTIONS: Questions 10 and 11 are based on the following layout.

Layout of Conference Room
BUREAU OF RODENT CONTROL

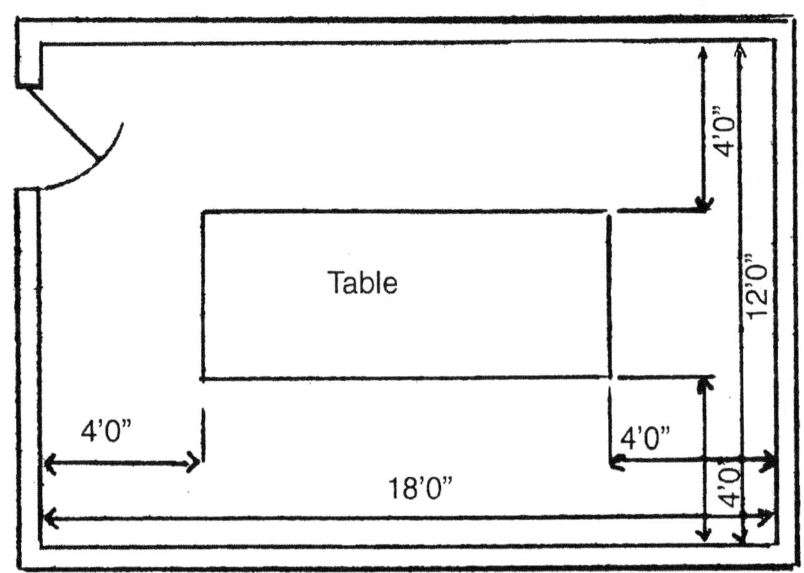

10. The LARGEST number of persons that can be accommodated in the area shown in the layout is 10._____

A. 16 B. 10 C. 8 D. 6

11. Assume that the Bureau's programs undergo expansion and the Director indicates that the feasibility of increasing the size of the conference room should be explored. 11._____
For every two additional persons that are to be accommodated, the analyst should recommend that ______ be added to table length and ______ be added to room length.

A. 2'-6";2'-6"
B. 5'-0"; 5'-0"
C. 2'-6"; 5'-0"
D. 5'-0"; 2'-6"

Questions 12-14.

DIRECTIONS: Questions 12 through 14 are based on the following information.

SYMBOLS USED IN LAYOUT WORK

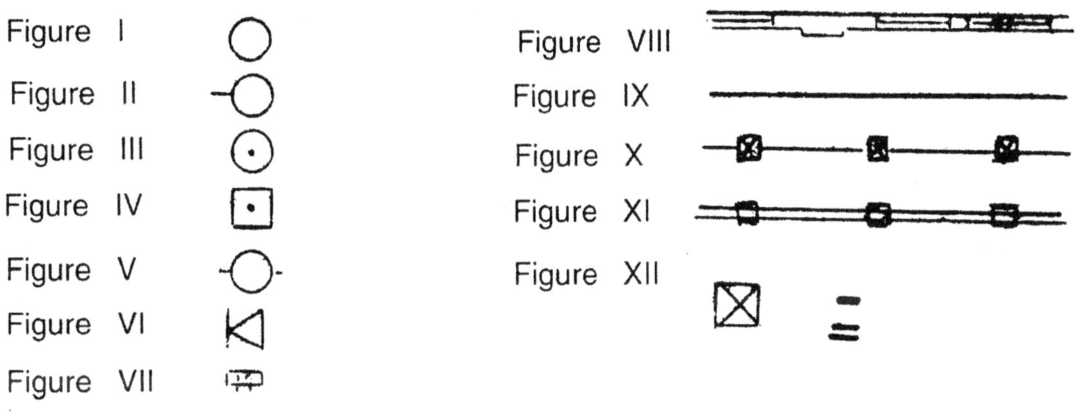

Figure I

Figure II

Figure III

Figure IV

Figure V

Figure VI

Figure VII

Figure VIII

Figure IX

Figure X

Figure XI

Figure XII

12. Figure XI is the symbol for 12.____

A. a temporary partition
B. floor outlets
C. ceiling outlets
D. a switch

13. A *solid post* is represented by Figure 13.____

A. II
B. V
C. VIII
D. XII

14. Figure VI is the symbol for a(n) 14.____

A. switch
B. intercom
C. telephone outlet
D. railing

15. While there is no one office layout that will fit all organizations, there are some reasonably good principles of office layout by function that could be applied to any office situation. 15.____
Which one of the following statements relating to functions and locations is MOST characteristic of a good layout?
The

A. personnel department is usually close to the reception area
B. purchasing department should be far from the entrance
C. data processing activity and duplicating services are normally placed together
D. top management group is usually dispersed throughout the general office group

16. Records are valuable to an organization becaused recorded information is more accurate and enduring than oral information. 16.____
Of the following, the MOST important stage in records management is at the

A. storage stage
B. time when quality control principles are applied
C. point of distribution
D. source when records are created

17. The rough layout of an office can be made by sketching the office floor plan from actual measurements, or it can be copied from blueprints furnished by the building management. 17.____

As an analyst assigned to improve an office layout, you should be aware that the experienced layout man prefers to make his sketch from

A. a blueprint because it eliminates the extra work in checking a sketch made from it
B. actual measurements because a blueprint is in a scale of 1/4 or 1/2 inch to a foot instead of the preferred 1/8 inch scale
C. a blueprint because he can always trust the blueprint
D. actual measurements because he has to sketch in the desks and other equipment

18. Planning the traffic flow and appropriate aisle space in an office are factors an analyst must consider in any desk arrangement. 18.____

Of the following, it is *generally* the MOST desirable practice to

A. deny requests to rearrange desks to give employees more working space if the space left for the aisle is more than needed for the traffic
B. figure operating space and the open file drawer separately from the allowance for the aisle if files must open into the aisle
C. conserve space by making the main aisle in an office no wider than 36 inches
D. disregard the length of feeders to an aisle in determining the width of the aisle

19. Code systems which are used to mark records for long- or short-term retention are easy to devise and use. 19.____

Accordingly, of the following situations, it would be MOST appropriate to use the *destroy code* for

A. information that calls for action within 90 days and for which no record is necessary thereafter
B. information that may be needed for evaluation of past agency activities
C. records which contain information that is readily available elsewhere
D. records that contain information necessary for audit requirements

20. Assume your agency is moving into new quarters and you will assist your superior in assigning space to the various offices. The offices will be air-conditioned. The interior of the space to be assigned is located away from windows. 20.____

Of the following, it is MOST appropriate for you to recommend that the interior of the space be set aside for

A. legal offices and confidential investigation sections
B. visitors to the agency
C. conference and training rooms
D. typing and stenographic pools

KEY (CORRECT ANSWERS)

1. D
2. A
3. A
4. B
5. D
6. C
7. A
8. C
9. A
10. B
11. A
12. A
13. D
14. C
15. A
16. D
17. D
18. B
19. C
20. C

EXAMINATION SECTION
TEST 1

DIRECTIONS: Each question or incomplete statement is followed by several suggested answers or completions. Select the one that BEST answers the question or completes the statement. *PRINT THE LETTER OF THE CORRECT ANSWER IN THE SPACE AT THE RIGHT.*

1. The MOST important factor in establishing a disciplinary policy in an organization is 1._A_

   A. consistency of application
   B. strict supervisors
   C. strong enforcement
   D. the degree of toughness or laxity

2. The FIRST step in planning a program is to 2._A_

   A. clearly define the objectives
   B. estimate the costs
   C. hire a program director
   D. solicit funds

3. The PRIMARY purpose of control in an organization is to 3._B_

   A. punish those who do not do their job well
   B. get people to do what is necessary to achieve an objective
   C. develop clearly stated rules and regulations
   D. regulate expenditures

4. After a procedures manual has been written and distributed, 4._A_

   A. continuous maintenance work is necessary to keep the manual current
   B. it is best to issue new manuals rather than make changes in the original manual
   C. no changes should be necessary
   D. only major changes should be considered

5. Of the following, the MOST important criterion of effective report writing is 5._C_

   A. eloquence of writing style
   B. the use of technical language
   C. to be brief and to the point
   D. to cover all details

6. The use of electronic data processing 6._D_

   A. has proven unsuccessful in most organizations
   B. has unquestionable advantages for all organizations
   C. is unnecessary in most organizations
   D. should be decided upon only after careful feasibility studies by individual organizations

7. Of the following methods, which would normally be MOST appropriate to validate a new aptitude test? 7._D_

   A. Concurrent
   B. Construct
   C. Content
   D. Predictive

8. The PRIMARY purpose of work measurement is to 8.____

   A. design and install a wage incentive program
   B. determine who should be promoted
   C. establish a yardstick to determine extent of progress
   D. set up a spirit of competition among employees

9. A hypothetical construct is BEST defined as an(any) 9.____

   A. speculation that a researcher wishes to articulate
   B. entity or process presumed to exist but currently unable to be observed
   C. explanation of what antecedent conditions lead to various consequences
   D. expression of the relationship between stimulus and response variables

10. Representative samples are 10.____

   A. always drawn from finite populations
   B. always drawn from infinite populations
   C. drawn in a random, unbiased manner and have the characteristics of the larger universe
   D. larger than stratified samples

11. Interval or equal-interval scales have 11.____

   A. an absolute or natural zero that has empirical meaning
   B. none of the characteristics of nominal and ordinal scales
   C. no validity
   D. the property that numerically equal distances on the scale represent equal distances in the property being measured

12. Protective techniques of obtaining and analyzing information from respondents are 12.____

   A. designed so that subjects will respond as frankly as possible
   B. easier to analyze than objective techniques
   C. forms of structured scales
   D. to be avoided at all costs

13. Of the following, which is NOT a descriptive research design? ______ study. 13.____

   A. Case
   B. Correlation
   C. Developmental
   D. Pretest-posttest

14. One method of testing hypotheses using available materials produced by institutions, organizations, and individuals is 14.____

   A. content analysis
   B. distance-cluster analysis
   C. semantic differential
   D. sociometric analysis

15. The MOST important difference between experimental research and ex post facto research is 15.B

A. analysis of data required
B. control of the variables
C. cost of the study
D. length of time required to conduct the study

16. *The public health department of a large city wishes to study the effect of different chemicals on the retardation of tooth decay in children. Three groups of children ranging in age from 10 to 15 are selected randomly. One group of children is given toothpaste containing chemical X and another group is given toothpaste with chemical Y. A third group is given toothpaste with no chemical added. All three groups are given the same kind of toothbrush and are asked to brush their teeth twice a day for one year using the toothpaste and toothbrushes they have received. Periodic dental check-ups are made of the children in all three groups to determine the amount of tooth decay.* 16.____
In the above study, the independent and dependent variables may BEST be defined as follows:

A. chemicals X and Y and toothbrushes are independent variables and the amount of tooth decay is the dependent variable
B. chemicals X and Y are independent variables and the amount of tooth decay is the dependent variable
C. chemicals X and Y, toothbrushes, and the number of times a day the children brush their teeth are dependent variables and the amount of tooth decay is the independent variable
D. chemicals X and Y, toothbrushes, and the number of times a day the children brush their teeth are independent variables and the amount of tooth decay is the dependent variable

17. A research hypothesis may BEST be defined as a(n) 17.____

A. problem statement concerning two or more unknown variables
B. speculation based on the researcher"s experience
C. statement of expectation concerning the relations between variables which can be tested
D. expository statement of the statistical procedure to be used in the research

18. A review of the literature is included in the research report PRIMARILY in order to 18.____

A. demonstrate the scope of the investigator's knowledge about the research problem
B. develop the theoretical foundation of the study
C. indicate the literature reviewed by the investigator in planning the study
D. save the reader time

19. The null hypothesis is a statistical proposition which states that 19.____

A. no explanation of differences between variables should be accepted completely
B. no differences exist between two or more sample means
C. no variable can be accurately measured
D. the real difference between the variables of the problem is greater than one would expect by chance

20. The following scores were obtained by an elementary mathematics class at the end of one year of instruction: 20.____

11	19	17
2	15	6
5	6	8

If the score of 8 were changed to 10, the mean(,)

A. and median of this group of data would change but the mode would remain the same
B. median, and mode would change
C. median, and mode would remain the same
D. of this group of data would change but the median would remain the same

21. The normal distribution which is represented by a theoretical bell-shaped curve has the following property: 21.____

A. Exactly .6826 of the total area will fall between an ordinate of two standard deviations above the mean
B. It is a fictional curve having no real function
C. The mean and median will coincide and have exactly the same value
D. The total area under the curve is equal to 2.98

22. In the case of variables that are linearly related, the correlation coefficient is a measure of 22.____

A. the causal relationship present between variables
B. the difference between the mean and the standard deviation
C. the direction and degree of the relationship between variables
D. which variable is independent and which is dependent

23. If a student's score on the final examination in a chemistry class is at the 72nd percentile, one can SAFELY assume that 23.____

A. the student answered 7 more questions correctly than did a student whose score was at the 65th percentile
B. 72% of the class scored lower than this student
C. the student answered 72 out of 100 questions correctly
D. the student is above average in chemistry

24. The significance level of a statistic is the probability that 24.____

A. a Type II error has been committed
B. the obtained result of the statistic could occur by chance
C. the outcome of the experiment is $\overline{X}_1 \neq \overline{X}_2$
D. there is a positive relationship between the variables being measured

25. The standard error of the mean is an estimate of 25.____

A. how far the sample mean is likely to differ from the population mean
B. how far two sample means differ from each other
C. the amount of error committed in computation
D. the amount of error inherent in the population mean

26. Nonparametric statistics are different from parametric statistics in that 26.____

    A. conditions about the population parameters are not specified in nonparametric tests
    B. nonparametric statistics are easier and faster to compute
    C. the measures to be analyzed by nonparametric tests must be continuous
    D. the measures to be analyzed by parametric statistics must be discrete

27. The Chi square test CANNOT be used reliably when the 27.____

    A. population distribution is not assumed to be normal
    B. population distribution is positively skewed
    C. samples are very large
    D. samples are very small

28. Of the following, the MOST critical problem faced by metropolitan educational systems is 28.____

    A. inadequate physical facilities
    B. parental indifference
    C. the lack of motivation to learn among urban youth
    D. the rapidity and magnitude of population change

29. In reference to educational systems, the concept of community control 29.____

    A. advocates that parents should take the place of professional educators
    B. implies that all educational decisions should be voted upon in open community meetings
    C. is essentially the same as decentralization
    D. represents the idea that the ultimate authority to make policy decisions rests with community representatives

30. Of the following, the MOST serious drawback to the *grant-in-aid* approach to support community services is that 30.____

    A. grants are difficult to obtain
    B. it encourages overcentralization of services
    C. it has had little or no provision for coordination of services
    D. it is too expensive

31. Of the following, the BEST definition of records management is 31.____

    A. storage of all types of records at minimum expense
    B. planned control of all types of records
    C. storage of records for maximum accessibility
    D. systematic filing of all types of records

32. The title of a contemporary best-selling book by Robert Townsend is . 32.____

    A. MANAGEMENT ANALYSIS: WAVE OF THE FUTURE
    B. MANAGEMENT FOR RESULTS
    C. THE HUMAN SIDE OF ENTERPRISE
    D. UP THE ORGANIZATION

33. A summary punched card containing totals of a group of similar detail cards is GENERALLY called a ______ card. 33.____

A. master unit record
B. summary unit record
C. total
D. unit record

34. One of the more famous studies of organizations is called the Hawthorne study. This work was one of the first to point out the importance of 34.____

A. employees' benefit and retirement programs
B. informal organization among employees
C. job engineering
D. styles of position classification

35. In organization theory, the type of position in which an individual is appointed to give technical aid to management on a particular problem area is generally BEST termed a(n) 35.____

A. administrative assistant
B. *assistant to*
C. staff assistant
D. staff specialist

36. In analyzing data for the acquisition of new equipment, a methods analyst gathers the facts, analyzes them, and develops new procedures which will be required when the new equipment arrives. 36.____
In analyzing the factors involved, which one of the following is normally LEAST important in the evaluation of new equipment?

A. Cost factors
B. Layout and installation factors
C. Production planning
D. Operational experience of manufacturers of allied equipment

37. The one of the following which is NOT a primary objective of a records retention and disposal system is to 37.____

A. assure appropriate preservation of records having permanent value
B. dispose of records not warranting further preservation
C. establish retention standards for archives
D. provide an opportunity to use miniaturization techniques to simplify filing systems

38. In organizing, doing what *works* in the particular situation, with due regard to both short and long range objectives, is BEST termed 38.____

A. ambivalence
B. authoritarianism
C. decentralization
D. pragmatism

39. If an effort were made to reduce the number of private offices in a new layout, the LEAST effective substitute in offering privacy would be the use of 39.____

A. an open area, with lower movable partitions or railings separating each individual
B. conference rooms
C. larger desks
D. modular desk units

40. The term *administrative substation* NORMALLY refers to 40.____

A. a work station handling a number of office services for an office organization
B. a work station where middle level supervisors are located
C. an office for handling management trainees
D. the functions allocated to particular levels of administrative managers

---

KEY (CORRECT ANSWERS)

1. A	11. D	21. C	31. B
2. A	12. A	22. C	32. D
3. B	13. D	23. B	33. B
4. A	14. A	24. B	34. B
5. C	15. B	25. A	35. D
6. D	16. B	26. A	36. D
7. D	17. C	27. D	37. D
8. C	18. B	28. D	38. D
9. B	19. B	29. D	39. C
10. C	20. A	30. C	40. A

TEST 2

DIRECTIONS: Each question or incomplete statement is followed by several suggested answers or completions. Select the one that BEST answers the question or completes the statement. *PRINT THE LETTER OF THE CORRECT ANSWER IN THE SPACE AT THE RIGHT.*

1. A research technique which would be applied to determine the optimum number of window clerks or interviewers to have in an agency serving the public would MOST likely be the use of 1.____

   A. line of balance B. queuing theory
   C. simulation D. work sampling

2. A type of file which permits the operator to remain seated while the file can be moved backward and forward as required is BEST termed a file. 2.____

   A. lateral B. movable
   C. reciprocating D. rotary

3. The technique of work measurement in which the analyst observes the work at random times of the day is BEST termed 3.____

   A. indirect observation B. logging
   C. ratio delay D. wristwatch

4. Examples of predetermined time systems generally should include all of the following EXCEPT 4.____

   A. Master Clerical Data B. Methods Time Measurement
   C. Short Interval Data D. Work Factor

5. A technique by which the supervisor or an assistant distributes a predetermined batch of work to the employees at periodic intervals of the day is generally BEST known as 5.____

   A. backlog control scheduling B. production control scheduling
   C. short interval scheduling D. workload balancing

6. Wright Bakke defined his *fusion process* as the 6.____

   A. work environment to some degree remakes the organization and the organization to some degree remakes the work environment
   B. fusing of the interests of both management and labor unions
   C. community of interest between first line supervisors and top management
   D. organization to some degree remakes the individual and the individual to some degree remakes the organization

7. If a staff analyst is required to recommend the selection of a machine for an office operation, he can BEST judge the expected output of a particular machine by pursuing which of the following courses of action? 7.____
   Obtaining

   A. an actual test run of the machine in his office
   B. data from the manufacturer of the machine
   C. information on the percentage of working time the machine will be used
   D. the experience of actual users of similar machines elsewhere

8. In planning office space for a newly established bureau, it would usually be LEAST desirable to 8.____

   A. concentrate, rather than disperse, the chief sources of office noises
   B. design an office environment with about the same brightness as the office desk
   C. designate as reception rooms, washrooms, and other service areas those areas that will receive lesser amounts of illumination than those areas in which private office work will be performed
   D. eliminate natural light in cases where it is not the major light source

9. A private office should be used when its use is dictated by facts and unbiased judgment. It should never be provided simply because requests and sometimes pressure have been brought to bear. 9.____
Of the following reasons used to justify use of a private office, the one that requires the MOST care in determining whether a private office is actually warranted is

   A. an office has always been provided for a particular job
   B. prestige considerations
   C. the confidential nature of the work
   D. the work involves high concentration

10. Theoretically, an ideal organization structure can be set up for each enterprise. In actual practice, the ideal organization structure is seldom, if ever, obtained. 10.____
Of the following, the one that normally is of LEAST influence in determining the organization structure is the

   A. existence of agreements and favors among members of the organization
   B. funds available
   C. opinions and beliefs of top executives
   D. tendency of management to discard established forms in favor of new forms

11. An IMPORTANT aspect to keep in mind during the decision-making process is that 11.____

   A. all possible alternatives for attaining goals should be sought out and considered
   B. considering various alternatives only leads to confusion
   C. once a decision has been made, it cannot be retracted
   D. there is only one correct method to reach any goal

12. Implementation of accountability requires 12.____

   A. a leader who will not hesitate to take punitive action
   B. an established system of communication from the bottom to the top
   C. explicit directives from leaders
   D. too much expense to justify it

13. Of the following, the MAJOR difference between systems and procedures analysis and work simplification is 13.____

   A. the former complicates organizational routine and the latter simplifies it
   B. the former is objective and the latter is subjective
   C. the former generally utilizes expert advice and the latter is a *do-it-yourself* improvement by supervisors and workers
   D. there is no difference other than in name

14. Systems development is concerned with providing 14._____

    A. a specific set of work procedures
    B. an overall framework to describe general relationships
    C. definitions of particular organizational functions
    D. organizational symbolism

15. Organizational systems and procedures should be 15._____

    A. developed as problems arise as no design can anticipate adequately the requirements of an organization
    B. developed jointly by experts in systems and procedures and the people who are responsible for implementing them
    C. developed solely by experts in systems and procedures
    D. eliminated whenever possible to save unnecessary expense

16. The CHIEF danger of a decentralized control system is that 16._____

    A. excessive reports and communications will be generated
    B. problem areas may not be detected readily
    C. the expense will become prohibitive
    D. this will result in too many *chiefs*

17. Of the following, management guides and controls clerical work PRINCIPALLY through 17._____

    A. close supervision and constant checking of personnel
    B. spot checking of clerical procedures
    C. strong sanctions for clerical supervisors
    D. the use of printed forms

18. Which of the following is MOST important before conducting fact-finding interviews? 18._____

    A. Becoming acquainted with all personnel to be interviewed
    B. Explaining the techniques you plan to use
    C. Explaining to the operating officials the purpose and scope of the study
    D. Orientation of the physical layout

19. Of the following, the one that is NOT essential in carrying out a comprehensive work improvement program is 19._____

    A. standards of performance
    B. supervisory training
    C. work count/task list
    D. work distribution chart

20. Which of the following control techniques is MOST useful on large, complex systems projects? 20._____

    A. A general work plan
    B. Gantt Chart
    C. Monthly progress report
    D. PERT Chart

21. The action which is MOST effective in gaining acceptance of a study by the agency which is being studied is 21.____

   A. a directive from the agency head to install a study based on recommendations included in a report
   B. a lecture-type presentation following approval of the procedures
   C. a written procedure in narrative form covering the proposed system with visual presentations and discussions
   D. procedural charts showing the *before* and *after* situation, forms, steps, etc. to the employees affected

22. Which of the following is NOT an advantage in the use of oral instructions as compared with written instructions? Oral instruction(s) 22.____

   A. can easily be changed
   B. is superior in transmitting complex directives
   C. facilitate exchange of information between a superior and his subordinate
   D. without discussions make it easier to ascertain understanding

23. Which organization principle is MOST closely related to procedural analysis and improvement? 23.____

   A. Duplication, overlapping, and conflict should be eliminated.
   B. Managerial authority should be clearly defined.
   C. The objectives of the organization should be clearly defined.
   D. Top management should be freed of burdensome detail.

24. Which of the following is the MAJOR objective of operational audits? 24.____

   A. Detecting fraud
   B. Determining organization problems
   C. Determining the number of personnel needed
   D. Recommending opportunities for improving operating and management practices

25. Of the following, the formalization of organization structure is BEST achieved by 25.____

   A. a narrative description of the plan of organization
   B. functional charts
   C. job descriptions together with organization charts
   D. multi-flow charts

26. Budget planning is MOST useful when it achieves 26.____

   A. cost control
   B. forecast of receipts
   C. performance review
   D. personnel reduction

27. The underlying principle of sound administration is to 27.____

   A. base administration on investigation of facts
   B. have plenty of resources available
   C. hire a strong administrator
   D. establish a broad policy

28. Although questionnaires are not the best survey tool the management analyst has to use, there are times when a good questionnaire can expedite the *fact-finding* phase of a management survey. 28.____
Which of the following should be AVOIDED in the design and distribution of the questionnaire?

A. Questions should be framed so that answers can be classified and tabulated for analysis.
B. Those receiving the questionnaire must be knowledgeable enough to accurately provide the information desired.
C. The questionnaire should enable the respondent to answer in a narrative manner.
D. The questionnaire should require a minimum amount of writing.

29. Of the following, the formula which is used to calculate the arithmetic mean from data grouped in a frequency distribution is 29.____

A. $M = \frac{N}{\Sigma fX}$
B. $M = N(\Sigma fX)$
C. $M = \frac{\Sigma fX}{N}$
D. $M = \frac{\Sigma X}{fN}$

30. Arranging large groups of numbers in frequency distributions 30.____

A. gives a more composite picture of the total group than a random listing
B. is misleading in most cases
C. is unnecessary in most instances
D. presents the data in a form whereby further manipulation of the group is eliminated

31. After a budget has been developed, it serves to 31.____

A. assist the accounting department in posting expenditures
B. measure the effectiveness of department managers
C. provide a yardstick against which actual costs are measured
D. provide the operating department with total expenditures to date

32. Of the following, which formula is used to determine staffing requirements? 32.____

A. $\frac{\text{Hours per man-day}}{\text{Volume X Standard}}$ = Employees Needed
B. $\frac{\text{Hours per man-day X Standard}}{\text{Volume}}$ = Employees Needed
C. $\frac{\text{Hours per man-day X Volume}}{\text{Standard}}$ = Employees Needed
D. $\frac{\text{Volume X Standard}}{\text{Hours per man-day}}$ = Employees Needed

33. Of the following, which formula is used to determine the number of days required to process work? 33.____

A. $\frac{\text{Employees X Daily Output}}{\text{Volume}}$=Days to Process Work

B. $\frac{\text{Employees X Volume}}{\text{Daily Output}}$=Days to Process Work

C. $\frac{\text{Volume}}{\text{Employees X Daily Output}}$=Days to Process Work

D. $\frac{\text{Volume X Daily Output}}{\text{Employees}}$=Days to Process Work

34. Identify this symbol, as used in a Systems Flow Chart. 34.____
   A. Document
   B. Decision
   C. Preparation
   D. Process

35. Of the following, the MAIN advantage of a form letter over a dictated letter is that a form letter 35.____
   A. is more expressive
   B. is neater
   C. may be mailed in a window envelope
   D. requires less secretarial time

36. The term that may be defined as a systematic analysis of all factors affecting work being done or all factors that will affect work to be done, in order to save effort, time or money is 36.____
   A. flow process charting
   B. work flow analysis
   C. work measurement
   D. work simplification

37. Generally, the LEAST important basic factor to be considered in developing office layout improvements is to locate 37.____
   A. office equipment, reference facilities, and files as close as practicable to those using them
   B. persons as close as practicable to the persons from whom they receive their work
   C. persons as close as practicable to windows and/or adequate ventilation
   D. persons who are friendly with each other close together to improve morale

38. Of the following, the one which is LEAST effective in reducing administrative costs is 38.____
   A. applying objective measurement techniques to determine the time required to perform a given task
   B. establishing budgets on the basis of historical performance data
   C. motivating supervisors and managers in the importance of cost reduction
   D. selecting the best method - manual, mechanical, or electronic - to process the essential work

39. *Fire-fighting* is a common expression in management terminology. 39.____
Of the following, which BEST describes *fire-fighting* as an analyst's approach to solving paperwork problems?

A. A complete review of all phases of the department's processing functions
B. A studied determination of the proper equipment to process the work
C. An analysis of each form that is being processed and the logical reasons for its processing
D. The solution of problems as they arise, usually at the request of operating personnel

40. Assume that an analyst with a proven record of accomplishment on many projects is having difficulties on his present assignment. 40.____
Of the following, the BEST course of action for his superior to take is to

A. assume there is a personality conflict involved and transfer the analyst to another project
B. give the analyst some time off
C. review the nature of the project to determine whether or not the analyst is equipped to handle the assignment
D. suggest that the analyst seek counseling

KEY (CORRECT ANSWERS)

1.	B	11.	A	21.	C	31.	C
2.	C	12.	B	22.	B	32.	D
3.	C	13.	C	23.	A	33.	C
4.	C	14.	B	24.	D	34.	A
5.	C	15.	B	25.	C	35.	D
6.	D	16.	B	26.	A	36.	D
7.	A	17.	D	27.	A	37.	D
8.	D	18.	C	28.	C	38.	B
9.	A	19.	B	29.	C	39.	D
10.	D	20.	D	30.	A	40.	C

EXAMINATION SECTION
TEST 1

DIRECTIONS: Each question or incomplete statement is followed by several suggested answers or completions. Select the one that *BEST* answers the question or completes the statement. *PRINT THE LETTER OF THE CORRECT ANSWER IN THE SPACE AT THE RIGHT.*

1. It is often desirable for an administrator to consult, during the planning process, the persons to be affected by those plans. 1.____
Of the following, the MAJOR justification for such consultation is that it recognizes the

   A. fact that participating in horizontal planning is almost always more effective than participating in vertical planning
   B. principle of participation and the need for a sense of belonging as a means of decreasing resistance and developing support
   C. principle that lower-level administrators normally are more likely than higher-level administrators to emphasize longer-range goals
   D. fact that final responsibility for the approval of plans should be placed in committees not individuals

2. In evaluating performance and, if necessary, correcting what is being done to assure attainment of results according to plan, it is *GENERALLY* best for the administrator to do which one of the following? 2.____

   A. Make a continual effort to increase the number of written control reports prepared.
   B. Thoroughly investigate in equal detail all possible deviations indicated by comparison of performance to expectation.
   C. Decentralize, within an operating unit or division, the responsibility for correcting deviations.
   D. Concentrate on the exceptions, or outstanding variations, from the expected results or standards

3. Generally, changes in the ways in which the supervisors and employees in an organization do things are MORE likely to be welcomed by them when the changes 3.____

   A. threaten the security of the supervisors than when they do not
   B. are inaugurated after prior change has been assimilated than when they are inaugurated before other major changes have been assimilated
   C. follow a series of failures in changes when they follow a series of successful changes
   D. are dictated by personal order rather than when they result from an application of previously established impersonal principles

4. For sound organizational relationships, of the following, it is generally MOST desirable that 4.____

   A. authority and responsibility be segregated from each other, in order to facilitate control
   B. the authority of a manager should be commensurate with his responsibility, and vice versa

C. authority be defined as the obligation of an individual to carry out assigned activities to the best of his or her ability
D. clear recognition be given to the fact that delegation of authority benefits only the manager who delegates it

5. In utilizing a checklist of questions for general managerial planning, which one of the following generally isthe FIRST question to be asked and answered? 5.____

A. Where will it take place?
B. How will it be done?
C. Why must it be done?
D. Who will do it?

6. Of the following, it is *USUALLY* best to set administrative objectives so that they are 6.____

A. at a level that is unattainable, so that administrators will continually be strongly motivated
B. at a level that is attainable, but requires some stretching and reaching by administrators trying to attain them
C. stated in qualitative rather than quantitative terms whenever a choice between the two is possible
D. stated in a general and unstructured manner, to permit each administrator maximum freedom in interpreting them

7. In selecting from among administrative alternatives, three general bases for decision are open to the manager experience, experimentation, and research and analysis. 7.____
Of the following, the best argument AGAINST primary reliance upon experimentation as the methods of evaluating administrative alternatives is that experimentation is

A. generally the most expensive of the three techniques
B. almost always legally prohibited in procedural matters
C. possible only in areas
D. where results may be easily duplicated by other experimenters at any time
E. an approach that requires information on scientific method seldom available to administrators

8. The administrator who utilizes the techniques of operations research, linear programming, and simulation in making an administrative decision should MOST appropriately be considered to be using the techniques of ______ analysis. 8.____

A. intuitive
B. quantitative
C. nonmathematical
D. qualitative

9. When an additional organizational level is added within a department, that department has MOST directly manifested 9.____

A. horizontal growth
B. horizontal shrinkage
C. vertical growth
D. vertical shrinkage

10. Of the following, the one which GENERALLY is the most intangible planning factor is 10._____

A. budget dollars allocated to a function
B. square feet of space for office use
C. number of personnel in various clerical titles
D. emotional impact of a proposed personnel policy among employees

11. Departmentation by function is the same as, or most similar to, departmentation by 11._____

A. equipment
B. clientele
C. territory
D. activity

12. Such verifiable factors as turnover, absenteeism, or volume of grievances would generally BEST assist in measuring the effectiveness of a program to improve 12._____

A. forms control
B. employee morale
C. linear programming
D. executive creativit

13. An organization increases the number of subordinates reporting to a manager up to the point where incremental savings in costs, better communication and morale, and other factors equal incremental losses in effectiveness of control, direction, and similar factors. This action MOST specifically employs the technique of 13._____

A. role playing
B. queuing theory
C. marginal analysis
D. capital standards analysis

14. The term *computer hardware* is MOST likely to refer to 14._____

A. machines and equipment
B. programmed instruction texts and compiler decks
C. training manuals
D. documentation supporting usage of computing machines

15. Determining what is being accomplished, that is, evaluating the performance and, if necessary, applying corrective measures so that performance takes place according to plans is MOST appropriately called management 15._____

A. actuating
B. planning
C. controlling
D. motivating

16. Of the following, the BEST overall technique for choosing from among several alternative public programs proposed to try to achieve the same broad objective generally is 16._____

A. random-sample analysis
B. input analysis
C. cost-effectiveness analysis
D. output analysis

17. When the success of a plan in achieving specific program objectives is measured against that plan's costs, the measure obtained is most directly that of the plan's 17._____

A. pervasiveness
B. control potential
C. primacy
D. efficiency

18. Generally, the degree to which an organization's planning will be coordinated varies MOST directly with the degree to which 18.____

    A. the individuals charged with executing plans are better compensated than those charged with developing and evaluating plans
    B. the individuals charged with planning understand and agree to utilize consistent planning premises
    C. a large number of position classification titles have been established for those individuals charged with organizational planning functions
    D. subordinate unit objectives are allowed to control the overall objectives of the departments of which such subordinate units are a part

19. The responsibility for specific types of decisions generally is BEST delegated to 19.____

    A. the highest organizational level at which there is an individual possessing the ability, desire, impartiality and access to relevant information needed to make these decisions
    B. the lowest organizational level at which there is an individual possessing the ability, desire, impartiality and access to relevant information needed to make these decisions
    C. a group of executives, rather than a single executive, if these decisions deal with an emergency
    D. The organizational level midway between that which will have to carry out these decisions and that which will have to authorize the resources for their implementation

20. The process of managing by objectives is MOST likely to lead to a situation in which the 20.____

    A. goal accomplishment objectives of managers tend to have a longer time span as one goes lower down the line in an organization
    B. establishment of quantitative goals for staff positions is generally easier than the establishment of quantitative goals for line positions
    C. development of objectives requires the manager to think of the way he will accomplish given results, and of the organization, personnel and resources that he will need
    D. superiors normally develop and finally approve detailed goals for subordinates without any prior consultation with either those subordinates or with the top-level executives responsible for the longer-run objectives of the organization

21. As used with respect to decision making, the application of scientific method to the study of alternatives in a problem situation, with a view to providing a quantitative basis for arriving at an optimum solution in terms of the goals sought is MOST appropriately called 21.____

    A. simple number departmentation
    B. geographic decentralization
    C. operations research
    D. trait rating

22. Assume that a bureau head proposes that final responsibility and authority for all planning within the bureau is to be delegated to one employee who is to be paid at the level of an assistant division head in that bureau.
Of the following, the MOST appropriate comment about this proposal is that it is 22.____

A. *improper;* mainly because planning does not call for someone at such a high level
B. *improper;* mainly because responsibility for a basic management function such as planning may not properly be delegated as proposed
C. *proper;* mainly because ultimate responsibility for all bureau planning is best placed as proposed
D. *proper;* mainly because every well-managed bureau should have a full-time planning officer

23. Of the following, the MOST important reason that participation has motivating effects is generally that it gives to the individual participating 23.____

A. a recognition of his desire to feel important and to contribute to achievement of worthwhile goals
B. an opportunity to participate in work that is beyond the scope of the class specification for his title
C. a secure knowledge that his organization's top leadership is as efficient as possible considering all major circumstances
D. the additional information which is likely to be crucial to his promotion

24. Of the following, the MOST essential characteristic of an effective employee suggestion system is that 24.____

A. suggestions be submitted upward through the chain of command
B. suggestions be acted upon promptly so that employees may be promptly informed of what happens to their submitted suggestions
C. suggesters be required to sign their names on the material sent to the actual evaluators for evaluation
D. suggesters receive at least 25% of the agency's savings during the first two years after their suggestions have been accepted and put into effect by the agency

25. Two organizations have the same basic objectives and the same total number of employees. The span of authority of each intermediate manager is narrower in one organization than it is in the other organization. It is MOST likely that the organization in which each intermediate manager has a narrower span of authority will have 25.____

A. fewer intermediate managers
B. more organizational levels
C. most managers reporting to a larger number of immediate supervisors
D. more characteristics of a *flat* organizational structure

KEY (CORRECT ANSWERS)

1. B
2. D
3. B
4. B
5. C
6. B
7. A
8. B
9. C
10. D
11. D
12. B
13. C
14. A
15. C
16. C
17. D
18. B
19. B
20. C
21. C
22. B
23. A
24. B
25. B

TEST 2

DIRECTIONS: Each question or incomplete statement is followed by several suggested answers or completions. Select the one that *BEST* answers the question or completes the statement. *PRINT THE LETTER OF THE CORRECT ANSWER IN THE SPACE AT THE RIGHT.*

1. Which one of the following BEST expresses the essence of the merit idea or system in public employment? 1.____

   A. A person's worth to the organization–the merit of his attributes and capacities–is the governing factor in his selection, assignment, pay, recognition, advancement and retention.
   B. Written tests of the objective type are the only fair way to select on a merit basis from among candidates for open-competitive appointment to positions within the merit system.
   C. Employees who have qualified for civil service positions shall have life-time tenure during good behavior in those positions regardless of changes in public programs.
   D. Periodic examinations with set date limits within which all persons desiring to demonstrate their merit may apply, shall be publicly advertised and held for all promotional titles.

2. Of the following, the promotion selection policy generally considered MOST antithetical to the merit concept is the promotion selection policy which 2.____

   A. is based solely on objective tests of competence
   B. is based solely on seniority
   C. may require a manager to lose his best employee to another part of the organization
   D. permits operating managers collectively to play a significant role in promotion decisions

3. Of the following, the problems encountered by government establishments which are MOST likely to make extensive delegation of authority difficult to effectuate tend to be problems of 3.____

   A. accountability and insuring uniform administration
   B. line and staff relationships within field offices
   C. generally employee opposition to such delegation of authority and to the subsequent record-keeping activities
   D. use of the management-by-objectives approach

4. The major decisions as to which jobs shall be created and who shall carry which responsibilities should GENERALLY be made by 4.____

   A. budgetary advisers
   B. line managers
   C. classification specialists
   D. peer-level rating committees

5. The ultimate controlling factor in structuring positions in the public service, MOST generally, should be the 5.____

A. possibility of providing upgrading for highly productive employees
B. collective bargaining demands initially made by established public employee unions
C. positive motivational effects upon productivity resulting from an inverted pyramid job structure
D. effectivenss of the structuring in serving the mission of the organization

6. Of the following, the most usual reason for UNSATISFACTORY line-staff relationships is 6.____

A. inept use of the abilities of staff personnel by line management
B. the higher salaries paid to line officials
C. excessive consultation between line officials and staff officials at the same organizational level
D. a feeling among the staff members thatv only lower-level line members appreciate their work

7. Generally, an employee receiving new information from a fellow employee is MOST likely to 7.____

A. forget the new information if it is consistent with his existing beliefs much more easily than he forgets the new information if it is inconsistent with his existing beliefs
B. accept the validity of the new information if it is consistent with his existing beliefs more readily than he accepts the validity of the new information if it is inconsistent with his existing beliefs
C. have a less accurate memory of the new information if it is consistent with his existing beliefs than he has of the new information if it is inconsistent with his existing beliefs.
D. ignore the new information if it is consistent with his existing beliefs more often than he ignores the new information if it is inconsistent with his existing beliefs

8. Virtually all of us use this principle in our human communications -- perhaps without realizing it. In casual conversations, we are alert for cues to whether we are understood (e.g., attentive nods from the other person). Similarly, an instructor is always interested in reactions among those to whom he is giving instruction. The effective administrator is equally conscious of the need to determine his subordinates' reactions to what he is trying to communicate. 8.____
The principle referred to in the above selection is MOST appropriately called

A. cognitive dissonance
B. feedback
C. negative reinforcement
D. noise transmission

9. Of the following, the PRINCIPAL function of an *ombudsman* generally is to 9.____

A. review departmental requests for new data processing equipment so as to reduce duplication
B. receive and investigate complaints from citizens who are displeased with the actions or non-actions of administrative officials and try to effectuate warranted remedies
C. review proposed departmental reorganizations in order to advise the chief executive whether or not they are in accordance with the latest principles of proper management structuring
D. presiding over courts of the judiciary convened to try *sitting* judges

10. Of the following, the MOST valid reason for recruiting an intermediate-level administrator from outside an agency, rather than from within the agency, normally is to 10.____

A. improve the public image of the agency as a desirable place in which to be employed
B. reduce the number of potential administrators who must be evaluated prior to filling the position
C. minimize the morale problems arising from frequent internal staff upgradings
D. obtain fresh ideas and a fresh viewpoint on agency problems

11. A group of positions that are sufficiently similar in nature and level of duties, responsibilities, and qualifications required to warrant similar treatment for purposes of recruitment, examination, and pay, is MOST appropriately called a(n) 11.____

A. grade
B. pay range
C. class
D. occupational group

12. Governmental personnel testing, MOST generally, has done which one of the following? 12.____

A. Shown greater precision in testing for creativity and courage than in testing for intelligence and achievement
B. Developed more useful tests of intelligence, aptitude and achievement than of creativity, courage, and commitment
C. Failed in the attempt to develop any testing mechanisms in the areas of aptitude or achievement to the point where they are of any use in eliminating extraneous, prejudicial factors in the selection process
D. Made more use of previous employment records in selecting novices from the outside for junior positions than it has in selecting persons from the outside to fill more senior positions

13. Of the following, the MAJOR objective of government managers in most job restructuring generally should be to 13.____

A. reduce the percentage that lower-level employees in the government service constitute of the total
B. reduce the percentage range of the salaries paid within each classified title
C. concentrate as much of the higher-skill duties in as few of the jobs as possible
D. package duties into job combinations that are the same as the job combinations traditionally used by lower-paying private employers in the surrounding geographical area

14. Which one of the following statements is MOST generally supported by modern industrial and behavioral research? 14.____

A. High productivity and high quality each show a substantial negative correlation with high morale.
B. Where professional employees participate in defining how much and what caliber of their service should be considered acceptable, they generally will set both types of goals substantially below those which management alone would have set.
C. Professional employees get greater satisfaction out of work that challenges them to exert their capacities fully.
D. The participative approach to management relieves the manager of the need to be a decision-maker.

15. The term *PPBS* relates MOST directly to one of the systems principally designed to do which one of the following? 15.____

A. Reduce the number of mistakes resulting in spoilage and wasted effort to zero
B. Obtain greater cost effectiveness
C. Assure that all operations are performed at the highest quality level that is technically attainable at the present time
D. Assure that all output units are fully verified prior to being sent out

16. Assume that you are working with a computer programmer to solve a complex problem. Together, you have defined your problem in everyday English clearly enough to proceed. In the next step, you both start breaking down the information in the definition so that you both can decide on the operations needed for programming the problem. This next step of getting from the definition *to* the problem to the point where you can begin laying out the steps actually to be taken in solving the problem is MOST appropriately called 16.____

A. completing the documentation
B. implementing the solution
C. identifying the problem statement
D. analyzing the problem

17. Assume that during the fiscal year 2006-2007, a bureau produced 20% more work units than it produced in the fiscal year 2005-2006. Also, assume that during the fiscal year 2006-2007 that bureau's staff was 20% SMALLER than it was in the fiscal year 2005-2006. 17.____
On the basis of this information, it would be most proper to conclude that the number of work units produced per staff member in that bureau in the fiscal year 2006-2007 exceeded the number of work units produced per staff member in that bureau in the fiscal year 2005-2006 by which one of the following percentages?

A. 20% B. 25% C. 40% D. 50%

18. Assume that during the following five fiscal years (FY), a bureau has received the following appropriations: 18.____
FY 1997-1998 - $200,000: FY 1998-1999 - $240,000
FY 1999-2000 - $280,000: FY 2000-2001 - $390,000
FY 2001-2002 - $505,000
The bureau's appropriation for which one of the following fiscal years showed the LARGEST percentage of increase over the bureau's appropriation for the immediately previous fiscal year?

A. FY 1998-1999
B. FY 1999-2000
C. FY 2000-2001
D. FY 2001-2002

19. A bureau has a very large number of clerical personnel engaged in very similar duties, and only a limited portion can be absent at any one time if the workload is to be handled properly. 19.____
Which one of the following would generally be the bureau head's BEST approach toward scheduling the annual leave time (vacations, etc.) to be taken by the employees of that bureau? The bureau head

A. personally receives from each employee his preferred schedule of annual leave time, personally decides on when the employee can most conveniently be spared from the Viewpoint of the office workload, and issues his decisions to all concerned in the form of a binding memorandum.
B. advises his subordinate supervisors and employees of the parameters and constraints in time and numbers upon annual leave. The employees and subordinate supervisors prepare a proposed annual leave schedule within those limitations and submit it to the bureau head for approval or modification, and for promulgation.
C. initially asks his subordinate supervisors to prepare a proposed annual leave schedule for employees with a minimum of consultation with the employees. He then circulates this schedule to the employees over his signature as a proposed schedule and invites reaction directly to him.
D. asks employee or union representatives to prepare a proposed schedule with all leave to be taken spread evenly over the entire vacation period. He personally reviews and accepts or modifies this proposal.

20. An agency head desires to have an estimate of the *potential* of a middle-level administrative employee for development for higher-level administrative positions. He also desires to try to minimize possible errors or capriciousness which might creep into that estimate. Of the following, it would generally be MOST desirable to have the estimate 20.____

A. result from the pooled judgment of three or more past or present substantial-level supervisors of the subject employee and of persons with lateral or service contracts with the subject employee
B. made solely by substantial-level executives outside the past or present direct line of supervision above the subject employee
C. result from the pooled judgment of substantial level personnel staff members rather than line executives
D. made solely by the present immediate line supervisor of the subject employee

21. Which one of the following generally BEST characterizes the basic nature of budget making and budget administration from a managerial viewpoint? 21.____

A. Budget administration is control, while budget making is planning.
B. Budget administration is planning, while budget making is control.
C. Both budget making and budget administration are only control functions; neither is a planning function.
D. Both budget making and budget administration are only planning functions; neither is a control function.

22. In preparing his annual budget request for a large bureau with both substantial continuing and anticipated new activities, the bureau head must consider various factors (e.g., retaining credibility and obtaining required funds). Of the following, the BEST long-range budgeting strategy would NORMALLY be for the bureau head to request 22.____

A. twice what is actually needed on the assumption that higher authorities will generally cut the requested amount in half
B. ten per cent less than he actually estimates to be needed and to submit a supplementary request later for that ten per cent
C. what is needed for the continuing activities plus twenty-five per cent to allow some slack funds

D. what he estimates is needed to continue existing essential programs and to fund needed new activities

23. If we total all of the occasions in which all governmental positions are filled with new faces (persons who did not occupy those specific positions previously), we generally would find that a GREATER number will result from 23.____

A. new accessions from the outside than from movement of personnel within the organization
B. movement of personnel within the organization than from new accessions from the outside
C. promotion of staff personnel to higher staff jobs than from promotion of line personnel to higher line jobs
D. filling of Exempt and Non-Competitive Class positions than from filling of Competitive Class positions

24. Listed immediately below are four measures to be utilized to try to achieve a major personnel goal: 24.____
(1) Diversifying tasks in any one unit as much as feasible
(2) Delegating authority to each layer in the hierarchy to the maximum extent cosistent with the clarity of policy guides, training of staff, and the effectiveness of post-audit procedures
(3) Assigning whole integrals of functions to individuals or units instead of splitting them into fine specializations with separate employees or groups concentrating on each
(4) Permitting workers to follow through on tasks or projects from start to finish rather than carry out single segments of the process
The major personnel goal which all of the above measures, taken together, may BEST be expected to serve is

A. increasing job simplification
B. promoting E.E.O. affirmative action
C. making and keeping jobs as meaningful as they can practically be
D. increasing the number of promotional levels available so as to maximize advancement opportunities as much as possible

25. Which one of the following is generally the BEST criterion for determining the classification title to which a position should be allocated? 25.____
The

A. personal qualifications possessed by the present or expected appointee to the position
B. consequences of the work of the position or the responsibility it carries
C. number of work units required to be produced or completed in the position
D. consequences of inadequate overall governmental pay scales upon recruitment of outstanding personnel

KEY (CORRECT ANSWERS)

1. A
2. B
3. A
4. B
5. D

6. A
7. B
8. B
9. B
10. D

11. C
12. B
13. C
14. C
15. B

16. D
17. D
18. C
19. B
20. A

21. A
22. D
23. B
24. C
25. B

EXAMINATION SECTION
TEST 1

DIRECTIONS: Each question or incomplete statement is followed by several suggested answers or completions. Select the one that BEST answers the question or completes the statement. *PRINT THE LETTER OF THE CORRECT ANSWER IN THE SPACE AT THE RIGHT.*

1. In many instances, managers deliberately set up procedures and routines that more than one department or more than one employee is required to complete and verify an entire operation or transaction. 1.____
   The MAIN reason for establishing such routines is *generally* to

   A. minimize the chances of gaps and deficiencies in feedback of information to management
   B. expand the individual employee's vision and concern for broader organizational objectives
   C. provide satisfaction of employees' social and egoistic needs through teamwork and horizontal communications
   D. facilitate internal control designed to prevent errors, whether intentional or accidental

2. Committees–sometimes referred to as boards, commissions, or task forces–are widely used in government to investigate certain problems or to manage certain agencies. 2.____
   Of the following, the MOST serious limitation of the committee approach to management in government is that

   A. it reflects government's inability to delegate authority effectively to individual executives
   B. committee members do not usually have similar backgrounds, experience, and abilities
   C. it promotes horizontal communication at the expense of vertical communication
   D. the spreading out of responsibility to a committee often results in a willingness to settle for weak, compromise solutions

3. Of the following, the BEST reason for replacing members of committees on a staggered or partial basis rather than replacing all members simultaneously is that this practice 3.____

   A. gives representatives of different interest groups a chance to contribute their ideas
   B. encourages continuity of policy since retained members are familiar with previous actions
   C. prevents interpersonal frictions from building up and hindering the work of the group
   D. improves the quality of the group's recommendations and decisions by stimulating development of new ideas

4. Assume that in considering a variety of actions to take to solve a given problem, a manager decides to take no action at all. 4.____
   According to generally accepted management practice, such a decision would be

A. *proper,* because under normal circumstances, it is better to make no decision
B. *improper,* because inaction would be rightly construed as shunning one's responsibilities
C. *proper,* since this would be a decision which might produce more positive results than the other alternatives
D. *improper,* since such a solution would delay corrective action and exacerbate the problem

5. Some writers in the field of management assume that when a newly promoted manager has been informed by his superior about the subordinates he is to direct and the extent of his authority, that is all that is necessary. However, thereafter, this new manager should realize that, for practical purposes, his authority will be effective ONLY when 5.____

A. he accepts full responsibility for the actions of his subordinates
B. his subordinates are motivated to carry out their assignments
C. it derives from acceptable personal attributes rather than from his official position
D. he exercises it in an authoritarian manner

6. A newly appointed manager is assigned to assist the head of a small developing agency handling innovative programs. Although this manager is a diligent worker, he does not delegate authority to middle- and lower-echelon supervisors. The MOST important reason why it would be desirable to change this attitude toward delegation is because otherwise 6.____

A. he may have to assume more responsibility for the actions of his subordinates than is implied in the authority delegated to him
B. his subordinates will tend to produce innovative solutions on their own
C. the agency will become a decentralized type of organization in which he cannot maintain adequate controls
D. he may not have time to perform other essential tasks

7. All types of organizations and all functions within them are to varying degrees affected today by the need to understand the application of computer systems to management practices. 7.____
The one of the following purposes for which such systems would be MOST useful is to

A. lower the costs of problem-solving by utilizing data that is already in the agency's control system correlated with new data
B. stabilize basic patterns of the organization into long-term structures and relationships
C. give instant solutions to complex problems
D. affect savings in labor costs for office tasks involving non-routine complex problems

8. Compared to individual decision-making, group decision-making is burdened with the DISADVANTAGE of 8.____

A. making snap judgments
B. pressure to examine all relevant elements of the problem
C. greater motivation needed to implement the decision
D. the need to clarify problems for the group participants

9. Assume that a manager in an agency, faced with a major administrative problem, has developed a number of alternative solutions to the problem. Which of the following would be MOST effective in helping the manager make the best decision? 9.____

   A. *Experience,* because a manager can distill from the past the fundamental reasons for success or failure since the future generally duplicates the past
   B. *Experimentation,* because it is the method used in scientific inquiry and can be tried out economically in limited areas
   C. *Research analysis,* because it is generally less costly than most other methods and involves the interrelationships among the more critical factors that bear upon the goal sought
   D. *Value forecasting,* because it assigns numerical significance to the values of alternative tangible and intangible choices and indicates the degree of risk involved in each choice

10. Management information systems operate more effectively for managers than mere data tabulating systems because information systems 10.____

   A. eliminate the need for managers to tell information processors what is required
   B. are used primarily for staff rather than line functions
   C. are less expensive to operate than manual methods of data collection
   D. present and utilize data in a meaningful form

11. Project-type organizations are in widespread use today because they offer a number of advantages. The MOST important purpose of the project organization is to 11.____

   A. secure a higher degree of coordination than could be obtained in a conventional line structure
   B. provide an orderly way of phasing projects in and out of organizations
   C. expedite routine administrative processes
   D. allow for rapid assessment of the status of any given project and its effect on agency productivity

12. A manager adjusts his plans for future activity by reviewing information about the performance of his subordinates. This is an application of the process of 12.____

   A. human factor impact
   B. coordinated response
   C. feedback communication
   D. reaction control

13. From the viewpoint of the manager in an agency, the one of the following which is the MOST constructive function of a status system or a rank system based on employee performance is that the system 13.____

   A. makes possible effective communication, thereby lessening social distances between organizational levels
   B. is helpful to employees of lesser ability because it provides them with an incentive to exceed their capacities
   C. encourages the employees to attain or exceed the goals set for them by the organization
   D. diminishes friction in assignment and work relation-ships of personnel

14. Some managers ask employees who have been newly hired by their agency and then assigned to their divisions or units such questions as: *What are your personal goals? What do you expect from your job? Why do you want to work for this organization?* For a manager to ask these questions is GENERALLY considered 14.____

A. *inadvisable;* these questions should have been asked prior to hiring the employee
B. *inadvisable;* the answers will arouse subjective prejudices in the manager before he sees what kind of work the employee can do
C. *advisable;* this approach indicates to the employee that the manager is interested in him as an individual
D. *advisable;* the manager can judge how much of a disparity exists between the employee's goals and the agency's goals

15. Assume that you have prepared a report to your superior recommending a reorganization of your staff to eliminate two levels of supervision. The total number of employees would remain the same, with the supervisors of the two eliminated levels taking on staff assignments. 15.____
In your report, which one of the following should NOT be listed as an expected result of such a reorganization?

A. Fewer breakdowns and distortions in communications to staff
B. Greater need for training
C. Broader opportunities for development of employee skills
D. Fewer employee errors due to exercise of closer supervision and control

16. *Administration* has often been criticized as being unproductive in the sense that it seems far removed from the end products of an organization. 16.____
According to modern management thought, this criticism, for the most part, is

A. *invalid,* because administrators make it possible for subordinates to produce goods or services by directing coordinating, and controlling their activities
B. *valid,* because most subordinates usually do the work required to produce goods and services with only general direction from their immediate superiors
C. *invalid,* because administrators must see to all of the details associated with the production of services
D. *valid,* because administrators generally work behind the scenes and are mainly concerned with long-range planning

17. A manager must be able to evaluate the relative importance of his decisions and establish priorities for carrying them out. 17.____
Which one of the following factors bearing on the relative importance of making a decision would indicate to a manager that he can delegate that decision to a subordinate or give it low priority? The

A. decision concerns a matter on which strict confiden-tiality must be maintained
B. community impact of the decision is great
C. decision can be easily changed
D. decision commits the agency to a heavy expenditure of funds

18. Suppose that you are responsible for reviewing and submitting to your superior the monthly reports from ten field auditors. Despite your repeated warnings to these auditors, most of them hand in their reports close to or after the deadline dates, so that you have no time to return them for revision and find yourself working overtime to make the necessary corrections yourself.
The deadline dates for the auditors' reports and your report cannot be changed.
Of the following, the MOST probable cause for this con-tinuing situation is that 18.____

A. these auditors need retraining in the writing of this type of report
B. possible disciplinary action as a result of the delay by the auditors has not been impressed upon them
C. the auditors have had an opportunity to provide you with feedback to explain the reasons for the delays
D. you, as the manager, have not used disciplinary measures of sufficient severity to change their behavior

19. Assume that an agency desiring to try out a *management-by-objectives* program has set down the guidelines listed below to implement this activity.
Which one of these guidelines is MOST likely to present obstacles to the success of this type of program? 19.____

A. Specific work objectives should be determined by top management for employees at all levels.
B. Objectives should be specific, attainable, and preferably measurable as to units, costs, ratios, time, etc.
C. Standards of performance should be either qualitative or quantitative, preferably quantitative.
D. There should be recognition and rewards for success-ful achievement of objectives.

20. Of the following, the MOST meaningful way to express productivity where employees work a standard number of hours each day is in terms of the relationship between man- 20.____

A. hours expended and number of work-units needed to produce the final product
B. days expended and goods and services produced
C. days and energy expended
D. days expended and number of workers

21. Agencies often develop productivity indices for many of their activities.
Of the following, the MOST important use for such indices is *generally* to 21.____

A. measure the agency's output against its own past performance
B. improve quality standards while letting productivity remain unchanged
C. compare outputs of the agency with outputs in private industry
D. determine manpower requirements

22. The MOST outstanding characteristic of staff authority, such as that of a public relations officer in an agency, as compared with line authority, is *generally* accepted to be 22.____

A. reliance upon personal attributes
B. direct relationship to the primary objectives of the organization
C. absence of the right to direct or command
D. responsibility for attention to technical details

23. In the traditional organization structure, there are often more barriers to upward communication than to downward communication. 23.____
From the viewpoint of a manager whose goal is to overcome obstacles to communication, this situation should be

A. *accepted;* the downward system is the more important since it is highly directive, giving necessary orders, instructions, and procedures
B. *changed;* the upward system should receive more emphasis than the downward system, which represents stifling bureaucratic authority
C. *accepted;* it is generally conceded that upward systems supply enough feedback for control purposes necessary to the organization's survival
D. *changed;* research has generally verified the need for an increase in upward communications to supply more information about employees' ideas, attitudes, and performance

24. A principal difficulty in productivity measurement for local government services is in defining and measuring output, a problem familiar to managers. A measurement that merely looks good, but which may be against the public interest, is another serious problem. Managers should avoid encouraging employees to take actions that lead to such measurements. 24.____
In accordance with the foregoing statement, it would be MOST desirable for a manager to develop a productivity measure that

A. correlates the actual productivity measure with impact on benefit to the citizenry
B. does not allow for a mandated annual increase in productivity
C. firmly fixes priorities for resource allocations
D. uses numerical output, by itself, in productivity incentive plans

25. For a manager, the MOST significant finding of the Hawthorne studies and experiments is that an employee's productivity is affected MOST favorably when the 25.____

A. importance of tasks is emphasized and there is a logical arrangement of work functions
B. physical surroundings and work conditions are improved
C. organization has a good public relations program
D. employee is given recognition and allowed to participate in decision-making

KEY (CORRECT ANSWERS)

1. D
2. D
3. B
4. C
5. B

6. D
7. A
8. D
9. C
10. D

11. A
12. C
13. C
14. A
15. D

16. A
17. C
18. D
19. A
20. B

21. A
22. C
23. D
24. A
25. D

TEST 2

DIRECTIONS: Each question or incomplete statement is followed by several suggested answers or completions. Select the one that BEST answers the question or completes the statement. *PRINT THE LETTER OF THE CORRECT ANSWER IN THE SPACE AT THE RIGHT.*

1. Which one of the following is generally accepted by managers as the MOST difficult aspect of a training program in staff supervision? 1.____

   A. Determining training needs of the staff
   B. Evaluating the effectiveness of the courses
   C. Locating capable instructors to teach the courses
   D. Finding adequate space and scheduling acceptable times for all participants

2. Assume that, as a manager, you have decided to start a job enrichment program with the purpose of making jobs more varied and interesting in an effort to increase the motivation of a certain group of workers in your division. Which one of the following should generally NOT be part of this program? 2.____

   A. Increasing the accountability of these individuals for their own work
   B. Granting additional authority or job freedom to these employees in their job activities
   C. Mandating increased monthly production goals for this group of employees
   D. Giving each of these employees a complete unit of work

3. Both employer and employee have an important stake in effective preparation for retirement. 3.____
   According to modern management thinking, the one of the following which is probably the MOST important aspect of a sound pre-retirement program is to

   A. make assignments that utilize the employee's abilities fully
   B. reassign the employee to a less demanding position in the organization for the last year or two he is on the job
   C. provide the employee with financial data and other facts that would be pertinent to his retirement planning
   D. encourage the employee to develop interests and hobbies which are connected with the job

4. The civil service system generally emphasizes a policy of *promotion-from-within.* 4.____
   Employees in the direct line of promotion in a given occupational group are eligible for promotion to the next higher title in that occupational group.
   Which one of the following is LEAST likely to occur as a result of this policy and practice?

   A. Training time will be saved since employees in higher-level positions are already familiar with many agency rules, regulations, and procedures.
   B. The recruitment section will be able to show prospective employees that there are distinct promotional opportunities.
   C. Employees will be provided with a clear-cut picture as to their possible career ladder.
   D. Employees will be encouraged to seek broad-based training and education to enhance their promotability.

5. From a management point of view, the MAIN drawback of seniority as opposed to merit as a basis for granting pay increases to workers is that a pay increase system based on seniority 5._____

   A. is favored by unions
   B. upsets organizational status relationships
   C. may encourage mediocre performance by employees
   D. is more difficult to administer than a merit plan

6. One of the actions that is often taken against employees in the non-uniformed forces who are accused of misconduct on the job is suspension without pay. 6._____
   The MOST justifiable reason for taking such action is to

   A. ease an employee out of the agency
   B. enable an investigation to be conducted into the circumstances of the offense where doubt exists about the guilt of the employee
   C. improve the performance of the employee when he returns to the job
   D. punish the employee by imposing a hardship on him

7. A manager has had difficulty in getting good clerical employees to staff a filing section under his supervision. To add to his problems, one of his most competent senior clerks requests a transfer to the accounting division so that he can utilize his new accounting skill, which he is acquiring by going to college at night. The manager attempts to keep the senior clerk in his filing section by calling the director of personnel and getting him to promise not to authorize any transfer. GENERALLY, this manager's action is 7._____

   A. *desirable;* he should not help his staff to develop themselves if it means losing good people
   B. *undesirable* ; he should recommend that the senior clerk get a raise in the hope of preventing him from transferring to another section
   C. *desirable;* it shows that the manager is concerned about the senior clerk's future performance
   D. *undesirable;* it is good policy to transfer employees to the type of work they are interested in and for which they are acquiring training

8. One of your subordinates, a unit supervisor, comes to you, the division chief, because he feels that he is working out of title, and he suggests that his competitive class position should be reclassified to a higher title. 8._____
   Which one of the following statements that the subordinate has made is generally LEAST likely to be a valid support for his suggestion?

   A. The work he is doing conforms to the general statement of duties and responsibilities as described in the class specification for the next higher title in his occupational group.
   B. Most of the typical tasks he performs are listed in the class specification for a title with a higher salary range and are not listed for his current title.
   C. His education and experience qualifications far exceed the minimum requirements for the position he holds.
   D. His duties and responsibilities have changed recently and are now similar to those of his supervisor.

9. Assume that a class specification for a competitive title used exclusively by your agency is outdated, and that no examination for the title has been given since the specification was issued. 9.___
Of the following, the MOST appropriate action for your agency to take is to

A. make the necessary changes and submit the revised class specification to the city civil service commission
B. write the personnel director to recommend that the class specification be updated, giving the reasons and suggested revisions
C. prepare a revised class specification and submit it to the office of management and budget for their approval
D. secure approval of the state civil service commission to update the class specification, and then submit the revised specification to the city civil service commission

10. Assume that an appropriate eligible list has been established and certified to your agency for a title in which a large number of provisionals are serving in your agency. In order to obtain permission from the personnel director to retain some of them beyond the usual time limit set by rules (two months) following certification of the list, which one of the following conditions MUST apply? 10.___

A. The positions are sensitive and require investigation of eligibles prior to appointment.
B. Replacement of all provisionals within two months would impair essential public service.
C. Employees are required to work rotating shifts, including nights and weekends.
D. The duties of the positions require unusual physical effort and endurance.

11. Under the federally-funded Comprehensive Employment and Training Act (CETA), the hiring by the city of non-civil servants for CETA jobs is PROHIBITED when the 11.___

A. applicants are unemployed because of seasonal lay-offs in private industry
B. applicants do not meet U.S. citizenship and city residence requirements
C. jobs have minimum requirements of specialized professional or technical training and experience
D. jobs are comparable to those performed by laid-off civil servants

12. Assume you are in charge of the duplicating service in your agency. Since employees assigned to this operation lack a sense of accomplishment because the work is highly specialized and repetitive, your superior proposes to enlarge the jobs of these workers and asks you about your reaction to this strategy. 12.___
The MOST appropriate response for you to make is that job enlargement would be

A. *undesirable,* PRIMARILY because it would increase production costs
B. *undesirable,* PRIMARILY because it would diminish the quality of the output
C. *desirable,* PRIMARILY because it might make it possible to add an entire level of management to the organizational structure of your agency
D. *desirable,* PRIMARILY because it might make it possible to decrease the amount of supervision the workers will require

13. According to civil service law, layoff or demotion must be made in inverse order of seniority among employees permanently serving in the same title and layoff unit. Which one of the following is now the CORRECT formula for computing seniority? 13.___
Total continuous service in the

A. competitive class *only*
B. competitive, non-competitive, or labor class
C. classified or unclassified services
D. competitive, non-competitive, exempt, and labor classes

14. Under which of the following conditions would an appoint-ing officer be permitted to consider the sex of a candidate in making an employment decision? When 14.____

A. the duties of the position require considerable physical effort or strength
B. the duties of the position are considered inherently dangerous
C. separate toilet facilities and dressing rooms for the sexes are unavailable and/or cannot be provided in any event
D. the public has indicated a preference to be served by persons of a specified sex

15. Assume that an accountant under your supervision signs out to the field to make an agency audit. It is later discovered that, although he had reported himself at work until 5 P.M. that day, he had actually left for home at 3:30 P.M. Although this accountant has worked for the city for ten years and has had an excellent performance record, he is demoted to a lower title in punishment for this breach of duty. 15.____
According to generally accepted thinking on personnel management, the disciplinary action taken in this case should be considered

A. *appropriate;* a lesser penalty might encourage repetition of the offense
B. *inappropriate;* the correct penalty for such a breach of duty should be dismissal
C. *appropriate;* the accountant's abilities may be utilized better in the new assignment
D. *inappropriate;* the impact of a continuing stigma and loss of salary is not commensurate with the offense committed

16. Line managers often request more funds for their units than are actually required to attain their current objectives. 16.____
Which one of the following is the MOST important reason for such inflated budget requests?
The

A. expectation that budget examiners will exercise their prerogative of budget cutting
B. line manager's interest in improving the performance of his unit is thereby indicated to top management
C. expectation that such requests will make it easier to obtain additional funds in future years
D. opinion that it makes sense to obtain additional funds and decide later how to use them

17. Integrating budgeting with program planning and evaluation in a city agency is GENERALLY considered to be 17.____

A. *undesirable;* budgeting must focus on the fiscal year at hand, whereas planning must concern itself with developments over a period of years
B. *desirable;* budgeting facilitates the choice-making process by evaluating the financial implications of agency programs and forcing cost comparisons among them
C. *undesirable;* accountants and statisticians with the required budgetary skills have little familiarity with the substantive programs that the agency is conducting
D. *desirable;* such a partnership increases the budgetary skills of planners, thus promoting more effective use of public resources

18. As an aspect of the managerial function, a budget is described BEST as a 18.___

A. set of qualitative management controls over productivity
B. tool based on historical accounting reports
C. type of management plan expressed in quantitative terms
D. precise estimate of future quantitative and qualitative contingencies

19. Which one of the following is *generally* accepted as the MAJOR immediate advantage of installing a system of program budgeting? 19.___
It

A. encourages managers to relate their decisions to the agency's long-range goals
B. is a replacement for the financial or fiscal budget
C. decreases the need for managers to make trade-offs in the decision-making process
D. helps to adjust budget figures to provide for unexpected developments

20. Of the following, the BEST means for assuring necessary responsiveness of a budgetary program to changing conditions is by 20.___

A. overestimating budgetary expenditures by 15% and assigning the excess to unforeseen problem areas
B. underestimating budgetary expenditures by at least 20% and setting aside a reserve account in the same amount
C. reviewing and revising the budget at regular intervals so that it retains its character as a current document
D. establishing *budget by exception* policies for each division in the agency

21. According to expert thought in the area of budgeting, participation in the preparation of a government agency's budget should GENERALLY involve 21.___

A. only top management
B. only lower levels of management
C. all levels of the organization
D. only a central budget office or bureau

22. Of the following, the MOST useful guide to analysis of budget estimates for the coming fiscal year is a com-parison with 22.___

A. appropriations as amended for the current fiscal year
B. manpower requirements for the previous two years
C. initial appropriations for the current fiscal year
D. budget estimates for the preceding five years

23. A manager assigned to analyze the costs and benefits associated with a program which the agency head proposes to undertake may encounter certain factors which cannot be measured in dollar terms. 23.___
In such a case, the manager should GENERALLY

A. ignore the factors which cannot be quantified
B. evaluate the factors in accordance with their degree of importance to the overall agency goals

C. give the factors weight equal to the weight given to measurable costs and benefits
D. assume that non-measurable costs and benefits will balance out against one another

24. If city employees believe that they are receiving adverse treatment in terms of training and disciplinary actions because of their national origin, they may file charges of discrimination with the Federal government's 24.____

A. Human Rights Commission
B. Public Employee Relations Board
C. Equal Employment Opportunity Commission
D. United States Department of Commerce

25. Under existing employment statutes, the city is obligated, as an employer, to take *affirmative action* in certain instances.
This requirement has been imposed to ensure that 25.____

A. employees who are members of minority groups, or women, be given special opportunities for training and promotion even though they are not available to other employees
B. employees or applicants for employment are treated without regard to race, color, religion, sex, or national origin
C. proof exists to show that the city has acted with good intentions in any case where it has disregarded this requirement
D. men and women are treated alike except where State law provides special hour or working conditions for women

---

KEY (CORRECT ANSWERS)

1. B
2. C
3. C
4. D
5. C
6. B
7. D
8. C
9. B
10. B
11. D
12. D
13. D
14. C
15. D
16. A
17. B
18. C
19. A
20. C
21. C
22. A
23. B
24. C
25. B

EXAMINATION SECTION
TEST 1

DIRECTIONS: Each question or incomplete statement is followed by several suggested answers or completions. Select the one that BEST answers the question or completes the statement. *PRINT THE LETTER OF THE CORRECT ANSWER IN THE SPACE AT THE RIGHT.*

1. An administrator in a department should be thoroughly familiar with modern methods of personnel administration. This statement is 1.____

   A. true, because this familiarity will help him in performing the normal functions of his office
   B. false, because personnel administration is not a departmental matter, but is centralized in the Civil Service Commission
   C. *true,* because this knowledge will insure the elimination of personnel problems in the department
   D. *false,* because departmental problems of a minor character are handled by the personnel representative, while major problems are the responsibility of the commissioner

2. The LEAST true of the following is that an administrative assistant in a department 2.____

   A. executes the policy laid down by the commissioner or his deputies
   B. in the main, carries out the policies of the commissioner but with some leeway where his own frame of reference is determinative
   C. is never required to formulate policy
   D. is responsible for the successful accomplishment of a section of the department's program

3. If a representative committee of employees in a large department is to meet with an administrative officer for the purpose of improving staff relations and of handling grievances, it is BEST that these meetings be held 3.____

   A. at regular intervals
   B. whenever requested by an aggrieved employee
   C. at the discretion of the administrative officer
   D. whenever the need arises

4. In the theory and practice of public administration, the one of the following which is LEAST generally regarded as a staff function is 4.____

   A. budgeting
   B. fire fighting
   C. purchasing
   D. research and information

5. The LEAST essential factor in the successful application of a service rating system is 5.____

   A. careful training of reporting officers
   B. provision for self–rating
   C. statistical analysis to check reliability
   D. utilization of objective standards of performance

6. Of the following, the one which is NOT an aim of service rating plans is 6.____

   A. establishment of a fair method of measuring employee value to the employer
   B. application of a uniform measurement to employees of the same class and grade performing similar functions
   C. application of a uniform measurement to employees of the same class and grade however different their assignments may be
   D. establishment of a scientific duties plan

7. A rule or regulation relating to the internal management of a department becomes effective 7.____

   A. only after it is filed in the office of the clerk
   B. as soon as issued by the department head
   C. only after it has been published officially
   D. when approved by the mayor

8. Of the following, the one MOST generally regarded as an *administrative* power is the 8.____

   A. veto power
   B. message power
   C. power of pardon
   D. rule making power

9. In public administration functional allocation involves 9.____

   A. integration and the assignment of administrative power
   B. the assignment of a single power to a single administrative level
   C. the distribution of a number of subsidiary responsibilities among all levels of government
   D. decentralization of administrative responsibilities

10. In the field of public administration, the LEAST general result of coordination is the 10.____

    A. performance of a well–rounded job
    B. elimination of jurisdictional overlapping
    C. performance of functions otherwise neglected
    D. elimination of duplication of work

11. Of the following, the MOST complicated and difficult problem confronting the reorganizer in the field of public administration is 11.____

    A. ridding the government of graft
    B. ridding the government of crude incompetence
    C. ridding the government of excessive decentralization
    D. conditioning organization to modern social and economic life

12. The *most accurate* description of the process of integration in the field of public administration is 12.____

    A. transfer of administrative authority from a lower to a higher level of government
    B. transfer of administrative authority from a higher to a lower level of government
    C. concentration of administrative authority within one level of government
    D. formal cooperation between city and state governments to administer a function

13. The one of the following who was *most closely* allied with *scientific management* is 13.____

A. Mosher B. Probst C. Taylor D. White

14. Of the following wall colors, the one which will reflect the GREATEST amount of light, other things being equal, is 14.____

A. buff B. light gray C. light blue D. brown

15. Natural illumination is LEAST necessary in a(n) 15.____

A. executive office
B. reception room
C. central stenographic bureau
D. conference room

16. The MOST desirable relative humidity in an office is 16.____

A. 30% B. 50% C. 70% D. 90%

17. When several pieces of correspondence are filed in the same folder they are *usually* arranged 17.____

A. according to subject
B. numerically
C. in the order in which they are received
D. alphabetically

18. Eliminating slack in work assignments is 18.____

A. speed-up
B. time study
C. motion study
D. efficient managment

19. *Time studies* examine and measure 19.____

A. past performance
B. present performance
C. long-run effect
D. influence of change

20. In making a position analysis for a duties classification, the one of the following factors which must be considered is the 20.____

A. capabilities of the incumbent
B. qualifications of the incumbent
C. efficiency attained by the incumbent
D. responsibility assigned to the incumbent

21. The MAXIMUM number of subordinates who can be effectively supervised by one administrative assistant is BEST considered as 21.____

A. determined by the law of *span of control*
B. determined by the law of *span of attention*
C. determined by the type of work supervised
D. fixed at not more than six

22. Of the following devices used in personnel administration, the MOST basic is 22.____

A. classification
B. service rating
C. appeals
D. in-service training

23. Of the following, the LEAST important factor for sound organization is the 23.____

A. individual and his position
B. hierarchical form of organization
C. location and delegation of authority
D. standardization of salary schedules

24. *Stretch–out* is a term that originated with the 24.____

A. imposition of a furlough
B. system of semi–monthly relief payments
C. development of labor technology
D. irregular development of low–cost housing projects

25. The one of the following which is LEAST generally true of a personnel division in a large department is that it is 25.____

A. concerned with having a certain point of view on personnel permeate the executive staff
B. charged with aiding operating executives with auxiliary staff service, assistance and advice
C. charged to administer a certain few operating duties of its own
D. charged with the basic responsibility for the efficient operation of the entire department

---

KEY (CORRECT ANSWERS)

1. A
2. C
3. A
4. B
5. B

6. D
7. B
8. D
9. C
10. C

11. D
12. C
13. C
14. A
15. B

16. A
17. C
18. D
19. B
20. D

21. C
22. A
23. D
24. C
25. D

TEST 2

Questions 1-10.

DIRECTIONS: Below are ten words numbered 1 through 10 and twenty other words divided into four groups - Group A, Group B, Group C and Group D. For each of the ten numbered words, select the word in one of the four groups which is MOST NEARLY the same in meaning. The letter of that group is the answer for the item. *PRINT THE LETTER OF THE CORRECT ANSWER IN THE SPACE AT THE RIGHT.*

1. abnegation 1.____
2. calumnious 2.____
3. purview 3.____
4. lugubrious 4.____
5. hegemony 5.____
6. arrogation 6.____
7. coalescence 7.____
8. prolix 8.____
9. syllogistic 9.____
10. contumely 10.____

GROUP A	GROUP B	GROUP C	GROUP D
articulation	bituminous	assumption	scope
fusion	deductive	forecast	vindication
catastrophic	repudiation	terse	amortization
inductive	doleful	insolence	productive
leadership	prolonged	panorama	slanderous

Questions 11-25.

DIRECTIONS: Each question or incomplete statement is followed by several suggested answers or completions. Select the one that BEST answers the question or completes the statement.

11. In large cities the total cost of government is of course *greater* than in small cities but 11.____
    A. this is accompanied by a decrease in per capita cost
    B. the per capita cost is also greater
    C. the per capita cost is approximately the same
    D. the per capita cost is considerably less in approximately 50% of the cases

12. The one of the following which is LEAST characteristic of governmental reorganizations is the 12.____
    A. saving of large sums of money
    B. problem of morale and personnel
    C. task of logic and management
    D. engineering approach

13. The LEAST accurate of the following statements about graphic presentation is 13.____

A. it is desirable to show as many coordinate lines as possible in a finished diagram
B. the horizontal scale should read from left to right and the vertical scale from top to bottom
C. when two or more curves are represented for comparison on the same chart, their zero lines should coincide
D. a percentage curve should not be used when the purpose is to show the actual amounts of increase or decrease

14. Grouping of figures in a frequency distribution results in a *loss* of 14.____

A. linearity B. significance C. detail D. coherence

15. The true financial condition of a city is BEST reflected when its accounting system is placed upon a(n) 15.____

A. cash basis B. accrual basis
C. fiscal basis D. warrant basis

16. When the discrepancy between the totals of a trial balance is $36, the LEAST probable cause of the error is 16.____

A. omission of an item
B. entering of an item on the wrong side of the ledger
C. a mistake in addition or subtraction
D. transposition of digits

17. For the *most effective* administrative management, appropriations should be 17.____

A. itemized B. lump sum C. annual D. bi-annual

18. Of the following types of expenditure control in the practice of fiscal management, the one which is LEAST important is that which relates to 18.____

A. past policy affecting expenditures
B. future policy affecting expenditures
C. prevention of improper use of funds
D. prevention of overdraft

19. The sinking fund method of retiring bonds does NOT 19.____

A. permit investment in a new issue of city bonds when the general market is unsatisfactory
B. cause irreparable injury to the city's credit when the city is unable to make a scheduled contribution
C. require periodic actuarial computations
D. cost as much to administer as the serial bond method

20. Of the following, the statement that is FALSE is: 20.____

A. Non-profit hospitalization plans are based on underlying principles similar to those which underlie mutual insurance
B. Federal, state and local governments pay for more than half of the medical care received by more than half of the population of the country
C. In addition to non-profit hospitalization, non-profit organizations providing reimbursement for medical and nursing care are now being organized in this state
D. Voluntary health insurance must be depended on since a state system of health insurance is unconstitutional

21. The *most accurate* of the following statements concerning birth and death rates is: 21.____

A. A high birth rate is usually accompanied by a relatively high death rate
B. A high birth rate is usually accompanied by a relatively low death rate
C. The rate of increase in population for a given area may be obtained by subtracting the death rate from the birth rate
D. The rate of increase in population for a given area may be obtained by subtracting the birth rate from the death rate

22. Empirical reasoning is based upon 22.____

A. experience and observation
B. *a priori* propositions
C. application of an established generalization
D. logical deduction

23. 45% of the employees of a certain department are enrolled in in-service training courses and 35% are registered in college courses. 23.____
The percentage of employees NOT enrolled in either of these types of courses is

A. 20%
B. at least 20% and not more than 55%
C. approximately 40%
D. none of these

24. A typist can address approximately R envelopes in a 7-hour day. A list containing S addresses is submitted with a request that all envelopes be typed within T hours. 24.____
The number of typists needed to complete this task would be

A. $\frac{7RS}{T}$
B. $\frac{S}{7RT}$
C. $\frac{R}{7ST}$
D. $\frac{7S}{RT}$

25. Bank X allows a customer to write without charge five checks per month for each $100 on deposit, but a check deposited or a cash deposit counts the same as a check written. Bank Y charges ten cents for every check written, requires no minimum balance and allows deposit of cash or of checks made out to customer free. A man receives two salary checks and, on the average, five other checks each month. He pays, on the average, twelve bills a month, five of which are for amounts between $5 and $10, five for amounts between $10 and $20, two for about $30. Assume that he pays these bills either by check or by Post Office money order (the charges for money orders are: $3.01 to $10–11¢; $10.01 to $20–13¢; $20.01 to $40–15¢) and that he has a savings account paying 2%. Assume also that if he has an account at Bank X, he keeps a balance sufficient to avoid any service charges. Of the following statements in relation to this man, the one that is TRUE is that 25.____

A. the monthly cost of an account at Bank Y is approximately as great as the cost of an account at Bank X and also the account is more convenient
B. to use an account at Bank Y costs more than the use of money orders, but this disadvantage is offset by the fact that cancelled checks act as receipts for bills paid
C. money orders are cheapest but this advantage is offset by the fact that one must go to the Post Office for each order
D. an account at Bank X is least expensive and has the advantage that checks endorsed to the customer may be deposited in it

---

KEY (CORRECT ANSWERS)

1. B
2. D
3. D
4. B
5. A

6. C
7. A
8. B
9. B
10. C

11. B
12. A
13. A
14. C
15. B

16. C
17. B
18. A
19. B
20. D

21. A
22. A
23. B
24. D
25. D

EXAMINATION SECTION
TEST 1

DIRECTIONS: Each question or incomplete statement is followed by several suggested answers or completions. Select the one that BEST answers the question or completes the statement. *PRINT THE LETTER OF THE CORRECT ANSWER IN THE SPACE AT THE RIGHT.*

1. The one of the following which has had GREATEST effect upon size of the budget of large cities in the last twenty years is 1.____

   A. change in the organization of the city resulting from new charters
   B. increase in services rendered by the city
   C. development of independent authorities
   D. increase in the city's ability to borrow money
   E. increase in the size of the city

2. The one of the following services for which cities receive the LEAST amount of direct financial assistance from state governments is 2.____

   A. education B. welfare C. housing D. roads E. museums

3. Major problems which face most large cities, including New York, arise from the vertical sandwiching of governments in a single area and from the many independent governments that crowd the boundaries of the central city. 3.____
   Of the following methods of solving these problems, the one which has been MOST successful in the past has been to

   A. decentralize the administration of the central city
   B. create various supra-municipal authorities which tend to integrate the activities of the metropolitan area
   C. bring the metropolitan population under a single local government
   D. set up intermunicipal coordinating agencies to solve area administrative and economic problems
   E. allow each government element in the metropolitan area to work out its own solution

4. By means of the *debt limit* the states regulate many facets of the debt of the cities. 4.____
   The one of the following factors which is NOT regulated in this manner is the

   A. purpose for which the debt is incurred
   B. amount of debt which may be incurred
   C. terms of the notes or bonds issued by the city
   D. forms of debts which may be incurred
   E. source from which the money may be borrowed

5. The one of the following which is a characteristic of NEITHER the state nor the Federal governments, but which is a characteristic of the government of cities is that the latter 5.____

   A. is not sovereign but an agent
   B. does not have the power to raise taxes
   C. cannot enter into contracts
   D. may not make treaties with foreign countries
   E. may not coin money

Questions 6-8.

DIRECTIONS: Questions 6 through 8 are based on the following paragraph:

The regressive uses of discipline are ubiquitous. Administrative architects who seek the optimum balance between structure and morale must accordingly look toward the identification and isolation of disciplinary elements. The whole range of disciplinary sanctions, from the reprimand to the dismissal, presents opportunities for reciprocity and accommodation of institutional interests. When rightly seized upon, these opportunities may provide the moment and the means for fruitful exercise of leadership and collaboration.

6. The one of the following ways of reworking the ideas presented in this paragraph in order to be BEST suited for presentation in an in-service training course in supervision is: 6.___

   A. When one of your men does something wrong, talk it over with him. Tell him what he should have done. This is a chance for you to show the man that you are on his side and that you would welcome him on your side.
   B. It is not necessary to reprimand or to dismiss an employee because he needs disciplining. The alert foreman will lead and collaborate with his subordinates making discipline unnecessary.
   C. A good way to lead the men you supervise is to take those opportunities which present themselves to use the whole range of disciplinary sanctions from reprimand to dismissal as a means for enforcing collaboration.
   D. Chances to punish a man in your squad should be welcomed as opportunities to show that you are a '*good guy*' who does not bear a grudge.
   E. Before you talk to a man or have him report to the office for something he has done wrong, attempt to lead him and get him to work with you. Tell him that his actions were wrong, that you expect him not to repeat the same wrong act, and that you will take a firmer stand if the act is repeated.

7. Of the following, the PRINCIPAL point made in the paragraph is that 7.___

   A. discipline is frequently used improperly
   B. it is possible to isolate the factors entering into a disciplinary situation
   C. identification of the disciplinary elements is desirable
   D. disciplinary situations may be used to the advantage of the organization
   E. obtaining the best relationship between organizational form and spirit, depends upon the ability to label disciplinary elements

8. The MOST novel idea presented in the paragraph is that 8.___

   A. discipline is rarely necessary
   B. discipline may be a joint action of man and supervisor
   C. there are disciplinary elements which may be identified
   D. a range of disciplinary sanctions exists
   E. it is desirable to seek for balance between structure and morale

9. When, in the process of developing a classification plan, it has been decided that certain positions all have distinguishing characteristics sufficiently similar to justify treating them alike in the process of selecting appointees and establishing pay rates or scales, then the kind of employment represented by such positions will be called a 'class'. 9.____
According to this paragraph, a group of positions is called a class if they

A. have distinguishing characteristics
B. represent a kind of employment
C. can be treated in the same mannner for some functions
D. all have the same pay rates
E. are treated in the same manner in the development of a classification plan

Questions 10–12.

DIRECTIONS: Questions 10 through 12 are based on the following paragraph:

The fundamental characteristic of the type of remote control which management needs to bridge the gap between itself and actual operations is the more effective use of records and reports–more specifically, the gathering and interpretation of the facts contained in records and reports. Facts, for management purposes, are those data (narrative and quantitative) which express in simple terms the current standing of the agency's program, work and resources in relation to the plans and policies formulated by management. They are those facts or measures (1) which permit management to compare current status with past performance and with its forecasts for the immediate future, and (2) which provide management with a reliable basis for long–range forecasting.

10. According to the above statement, a characteristic of a type of management control 10.____

A. is the kind of facts contained in records and reports
B. is narrative and quantitative data
C. is its remoteness from actual operations
D. is the use of records
E. which expresses in simple terms the current standing of the agency's program, provides management with a reliable basis for long-range forecasting

11. For management purposes, facts are, according to the paragraph 11.____

A. forecasts which can be compared to current status
B. data which can be used for certain control purposes
C. a fundamental characteristic of a type of remote control
D. the data contained in records and reports
E. data (narrative and quantitative) which describe the plans and policies formulated by management

12. An inference which can be drawn from this statement is that 12.___

A. management which has a reliable basis for long–range forecasting has at its disposal a type of remote control which is needed to bridge the gap between itself and actual operations
B. data which do not express in simple terms the current standing of the agency's program, work and resources in relationship to the plans and policies formulated by management, may still be facts for management purposes
C. data which express relationships among the agency's program, work and resources are management facts
D. the gap between management and actual operations can only be bridged by characteristics which are fundamentally a type of remote control
E. management compares current status with past performance in order to obtain a reliable basis for long–range forecasting

Questions 13–14.

DIRECTIONS: Questions 13 and 14 are based on the following paragraph:

People must be selected to do the tasks involved and must be placed on a payroll in jobs fairly priced. Each of these people must be assigned those tasks which he can perform best; the work of each must be appraised, and good and poor work singled out appropriately. Skill in performing assigned tasks must be developed, and the total work situation must be conducive to sustained high performance. Finally, employees must be separated from the work force either voluntarily or involuntarily because of inefficient or unsatisfactory performance or because of curtailment of organizational activities.

13. A personnel function which is NOT included in the above description is 13.___

A. classification
B. training
C. placement
D. severance
E. service rating

14. The underlying implied purpose of the policy enunciated in the above paragraph is 14.___

A. to plan for the curtailment of the organizational program when it becomes necessary
B. to single out appropriate skill in performing assigned tasks
C. to develop and maintain a high level of performance by employees
D. that training employees in relation to the total work situation is essential if good and poor work are to be singled out
E. that equal money for equal work results in a total work situation which insures proper appraisal

15. Changes in program must be quickly and effectively translated into organizational adjustments if the administrative machinery is to be fully adapted to current operating needs. Continuous administrative planning is indispensable to the successful and expeditious accomplishment of such organization changes. 15.____
According to this statement,

A. the absence of continuous administrative planning must result in out–moded administrative machinery
B. continuous administrative planning is necessary for changes in program
C. if changes in program are quickly and effectively translated into organizational adjustments, the administrative machinery is fully adapted to current operating needs
D. continuous administrative planning results in successful and expeditious accomplishment of organization changes
E. if administrative machinery is not fully adapted to current operating needs, then continuous administrative planning is absent

16. The first line supervisor executes policy as elsewhere formulated. He does not make policy. He is the element of the administrative structure closest to the employee group. 16.____
From this point of view, it follows that a MAJOR function of the first line supervisor is to

A. suggest desirable changes in procedure to top management
B. prepare time schedules showing when his unit will complete a piece of work so that it will dovetail with the requirements of other units
C. humanize policy so as to respect employee needs and interests
D. report danger points to top management in order to forestall possible bottlenecks
E. discipline employees who continuously break departmental rules

17. During a supervisory staff meeting, the department head said to the first line supervisors, *"The most important job you have is to get across to the employees in your units the desirability of achieving our department's aims and the importance of the jobs they are performing toward reaching our goals."* 17.____
In general, adoption of this point of view would tend to result in an organization

A. in which supervisors would be faced by many disciplinary problems caused by employee reaction to the program
B. in which less supervision is required of the work of the average employee
C. having more clearly defined avenues of communication
D. lacking definition; supervisors would tend to forget their primary mission of getting the assigned work completed as efficiently as possible
E. in which most employees would be capable of taking over a supervisory position when necessary

18. A supervisor, in assigning a man to a job, generally followed the policy of fitting the man to the job. 18.____
This procedure is

A. *undesirable;* the job should be fitted to the man
B. *desirable;* primary emplasis should be on the work to be accomplished
C. *undesirable;* the policy does not consider human values
D. *desirable;* setting up a definite policy and following it permits careful analysis
E. *undesirable;* it is not always possible to fit the available man to the job

19. Assume that one of the units under your jurisdiction has 40 typists. Their skill ranges from 15 to 80 words a minute. The MOST feasible of the following methods to increase the typing output of this unit is to 19.____

A. study the various typing jobs to determine the skill requirements for each type of work and assign to each typist tasks commensurate with her skill
B. assign the slow typists to clerical work and hire new typists
C. assign such tasks as typing straight copy to the slower typists
D. reduce the skill requirements necessary to produce a satisfactory quantity of work
E. simplify procedures and keep reports, memoranda and letters short and concise

20. In a division of a department, private secretaries were assigned to members of the technical staff since each required a secretary who was familiar with his particular field and who could handle various routine matters without referring to anyone. Other members of the staff depended for their dictation and typing work upon a small pool consisting of two stenographers and two typists. Because of turnover and the difficulty of recruiting new stenographers and typists, the pool had to be discontinued. 20.____
Of the following, the MOST satisfactory way to provide stenographic and typing service for the division is to

A. organize the private secretaries into a decentralized pool under the direction of a supervisor to whom nontechnical staff members would send requests for stenographic and typing assistance
B. organize the private secretaries into a central pool under the direction of a supervisor to whom all staff members would send requests for stenographic and typing assistance
C. train clerks as typists and typists as stenographers
D. relieve stenographers and typists of jobs that can be done by messengers or clerks
E. conserve time by using such devices as indicating minor corrections on a final draft in such a way that they can be erased and by using duplicating machines to eliminate typing many copies

21. Even under perfect organizational conditions, the relationships between the line units and the units charged with budget planning and personnel management may be precarious at times. 21.____
The one of the following which is a MAJOR reason for this is that

A. service units assist the head of the agency in formulating and executing policies
B. line units frequently find lines of communication to the agency head blocked by service units
C. there is a natural antagonism between planners and doers
D. service units tend to become line in attitude and emphasis, and to conflict with operating units
E. service units tend to function apart from the operating units

22. The one of the following which is the CHIEF reason for training supervisors is that 22.____

A. untrained supervisors find it difficult to train their subordinates
B. most persons do not start as supervisors and consequently are in need of supervisory training
C. training permits a higher degree of decentralization of the decision-making process
D. training permits a higher degree of centralization of the decision-making process
E. coordinated actions on the part of many persons pre-supposes familiarity with the procedures to be employed

23. The problem of determining the type of organization which should exist is inextricably interwoven with the problem of recruitment. In general, this statement is 23.____

A. *correct;* since organizations are man–made they can be changed
B. *incorrect;* the organizational form which is most desirable is independent of the persons involved
C. *correct;* the problem of organization cannot be considered apart from employee qualifications
D. *incorrect;* organizational problems can be separated into many parts and recruitment is important in only few of these
E. *correct; a* good recruitment program will reduce the problems of organization

24. The conference as an administrative tool is MOST valuable for solving problems which 24.____

A. are simple and within a familiar frame of reference
B. are of long standing
C. are novel and complex
D. are not solvable
E. require immediate solution

25. Of the following, a recognized procedure for avoiding conflicts in the delegation of authority is to 25.____

A. delegate authority so as to preserve control by top management
B. provide for a workable span of control
C. preview all assignments periodically
D. assign all related work to the same control
E. use the linear method of assignment

KEY (CORRECT ANSWERS)

1. B
2. E
3. C
4. E
5. A

6. A
7. D
8. B
9. C
10. D

11. B
12. A
13. A
14. C
15. A

16. C
17. B
18. B
19. A
20. A

21. D
22. C
23. C
24. C
25. D

TEST 2

DIRECTIONS: Each question or incomplete statement is followed by several suggested answers or completions. Select the one that BEST answers the question or completes the statement. *PRINT THE LETTER OF THE CORRECT ANSWER IN THE SPACE AT THE RIGHT.*

1. A danger which exists in any organization as complex as that required for administration of a large city is that each department comes to believe that it exists for its own sake. The one of the following which has been attempted in some organizations as a cure for this condition is to 1.____

   A. build up the departmental esprit de corps
   B. expand the functions and jurisdictions of the various departments so that better integration is possible
   C. develop a body of specialists in the various subject matter fields which cut across departmental lines
   D. delegate authority to the lowest possible echelon
   E. systematically transfer administrative personnel from one department to another

2. At best, the organization chart is ordinarily and necessarily an idealized picture of the intent of top management, a reflection of hopes and aims rather than a photograph of the operating facts within the organization. 2.____
   The one of the following which is the BASIC reason for this is that the organization chart

   A. does not show the flow of work within the organization
   B. speaks in terms of positions rather than of live employees
   C. frequently contains unresolved internal ambiguities
   D. is a record of past organization or of proposed future organization and never a photograph of the living organization
   E. does not label the jurisdiction assigned to each component unit

3. The drag of inadequacy is always downward. The need in administration is always for the reverse; for a department head to project his thinking to the city level, for the unit chief to try to see the problems of the department. 3.____
   The inability of a city administration to recruit administrators who can satisfy this need usually results in departments characterized by

   A. disorganization
   B. poor supervision
   C. circumscribed viewpoints
   D. poor public relations
   E. a lack of programs

4. When as a result of a shift in public sentiment, the elective officers of a city are changed, is it desirable for career administrators to shift ground without performing any illegal or dishonest act in order to conform to the policies of the new elective officers? 4.____

   A. *No;* the opinions and beliefs of the career officials are the result of long experience in administration and are more reliable than those of politicians
   B. *Yes;* only in this way can citizens, political officials and career administrators alike have confidence in the performance of their respective functions

C. *No;* a top career official who is so spineless as to change his views or procedures as a result of public opinion is of little value to the public service
D. *Yes;* legal or illegal, it is necessary that a city employee carry out the orders of his superior officers
E. *No;* shifting ground with every change in administration will preclude the use of a constant overall policy

5. Participation in developing plans which will affect levels in the organization in addition to his own, will contribute to an individual's understanding of the entire system. When possible, this should be encouraged. 5.____
This policy is, in general,

A. *desirable;* the maintenance of any organization depends upon individual understanding
B. *undesirable;* employees should participate only in those activities which affect their own level, otherwise conflicts in authority may arise
C. *desirable;* an employee's will to contribute to the maintenance of an organization depends to a great extent on the level which he occupies
D. *undesirable;* employees can be trained more efficiently and economically in an organized training program than by participating in plan development
E. *desirable;* it will enable the employee to make intelligent suggestions for adjustment of the plan in the future

6. Constant study should be made of the information contained in reports to isolate those elements of experience which are static, those which are variable and repetitive, and those which are variable and due to chance. 6.____
Knowledge of those elements of experience in his organization which are static or constant will enable the operating official to

A. fix responsibility for their supervision at a lower level
B. revise the procedure in order to make the elements variable
C. arrange for follow–up and periodic adjustment
D. bring related data together
E. provide a frame of reference within which detailed standards for measurement can be installed

7. A chief staff officer, serving as one of the immediate advisors to the department head, has demonstrated a special capacity for achieving internal agreements and for sound judgment. As a result he has been used more and more as a source of counsel and assistance by the department head. Other staff officers and line officials as well have discovered that it is wise for them to check with this colleague in advance on all problematical matters handed up to the department head. 7.____
Developments such as this are

A. *undesirable;* they disrupt the normal lines for flow of work in an organization
B. *desirable;* they allow an organization to make the most of its strength wherever such strength resides
C. *undesirable;* they tend to undermine the authority of the department head and put it in the hands of a staff officer who does not have the responsibility
D. *desirable;* they tend to resolve internal ambiguities in organization
E. *undesirable;* they make for bad morale by causing *cut throat* competition

8. A common difference among executives is that some are not content unless they are out in front in everything that concerns their organization, while others prefer to run things by pulling strings, by putting others out in front and by stepping into the breach only when necessary. 8.____
Generally speaking, an advantage this latter method of operation has over the former is that it

   A. results in a higher level of morale over a sustained period of time
   B. gets results by exhortation and direct stimulus
   C. makes it unnecessary to calculate integrated moves
   D. makes the personality of the executive felt further down the line
   E. results in the executive getting the reputation for being a good fellow

9. Administrators frequently have to get facts by interviewing people. Although the interview is a legitimate fact gathering technique, it has definite limitations which should not be overlooked. 9.____
The one of the following which is an important limitation is that

   A. people who are interviewed frequently answer questions with guesses rather than admit their ignorance
   B. it is a poor way to discover the general attitude and thinking of supervisors interviewed
   C. people sometimes hesitate to give information during an interview which they will submit in written form
   D. it is a poor way to discover how well employees understand departmental policies
   E. the material obtained from the interview can usually be obtained at lower cost from existing records

10. It is desirable and advantageous to leave a maximum measure of planning responsibility to operating agencies or units, rather than to remove the responsibility to a central planning staff agency. 10.____
Adoption of the former policy (decentralized planning) would lead to

   A. *less* effective planning; operating personnel do not have the time to make long–term plans
   B. *more* effective planning; operating units are usually better equipped technically than any staff agency and consequently are in a better position to set up valid plans
   C. *less* effective planning; a central planning agency has a more objective point of view than any operating agency can achieve
   D. *more* effective planning; plans are conceived in terms of the existing situation and their execution is carried out with the will to succeed
   E. *less* effective planning; there is little or no opportunity to check deviation from plans in the proposed set-up

Questions 11-15.

DIRECTIONS: The following sections appeared in a report on the work production of two bureaus of a department.

Base your answer to questions 11 through 15 on this information.

Throughout the report, assume that each month has 4 weeks.

Each of the two bureaus maintains a chronological file. In Bureau A, every 9 months on the average, this material fills a standard legal size file cabinet sufficient for 12,000 work units. In Bureau B, the same type of cabinet is filled in 18 months. Each bureau maintains three complete years of information plus a current file. When the current file cabinet is filled, the cabinet containing the oldest material is emptied, the contents disposed of and the cabinet used for current material. The similarity of these operations makes it possible to consolidate these files with little effort.

Study of the practice of using typists as filing clerks for periods when there is no typing work showed (1) Bureau A has for the past 6 months completed a total of 1500 filing work units a week using on the average 200 man–hours of trained file clerk time and 20 man–hours of typist time (2) Bureau B has in the same period completed a total of 2000 filing work units a week using on the average 125 man–hours of trained file clerk time and 60 hours of typist time. This includes all work in chronological files. Assuming that all clerks work at the same speed and that all typists work at the same speed, this indicates that work other than filing should be found for typists or that they should be given some training in the filing procedures used... It should be noted that Bureau A has not been producing the 1,600 units of technical (not filing) work per 30 day period required by Schedule K, but is at present 200 units behind. The Bureau should be allowed 3 working days to get on schedule.

11. What percentage (approximate) of the total number of filing work units completed in both units consists of the work involved in the maintenance of the chronological files? 11.___

    A. 5% B. 10% C. 15% D. 20% E. 25%

12. If the two chronological files are consolidated, the number of months which should be allowed for filling a cabinet is 12.___

    A. 2 B. 4 C. 6 D. 8 E. 14

13. The MAXIMUM number of file cabinets which can be released for other uses as a result of the consolidation recommended is 13.___

    A. 0 B. 1 C. 2 D. 3
    E. not determinable on the basis of the data given

14. If all the filing work for both units is consolidated without any diminution in the amount to be done and all filing work is done by trained file clerks, the number of clerks required (35–hour work week) is 14.___

    A. 4 B. 5 C. 6 D. 7 E. 8

15. In order to comply with the recommendation with respect to Schedule K, the present work production of Bureau A must be increased by 15.___

    A. 50% B. 100% C. 150% D. 200%
    E. an amount which is not determinable on the basis of the data given

16. A certain training program during World War II resulted in training of thousands of supervisors in industry. The methods of this program were later successfully applied in various governmental agencies. The program was based upon the assumption that there is an irreducible minimum of three supervisory skills. 16.____
The one of these skills among the following is

A. to know how to perform the job at hand well
B. to be able to deal personally with workers, especially face to face
C. to be able to imbue workers with the will to perform the job well
D. to know the kind of work that is done by one's unit and the policies and procedures of one's agency
E. the "know-how" of administrative and supervisory processes

17. A comment made by an employee about a training course was, *We never have any idea how we are getting along in that course.* The fundamental error in training methods to which this criticism points is 17.____

A. insufficient student participation
B. failure to develop a feeling of need or active want for the material being presented
C. the training sessions may be too long
D. no attempt may have been made to connect the new material with what was already known
E. no goals have been set for the students

18. Assume that you are attending a departmental conference on efficiency ratings at which it is proposed that a man–to–man rating scale be introduced. 18.____
You should point out that, of the following, the CHIEF weakness of the man–to–man rating scale is that

A. it involves abstract numbers rather than concrete employee characteristics
B. judges are unable to select their own standards for comparison
C. the standard for comparison shifts from man to man for each person rated
D. not every person rated is given the opportunity to serve as a standard for comparison
E. standards for comparison will vary from judge to judge

19. Assume that you are conferring with a supervisor who has assigned to his subordinates efficiency ratings which you believe to be generally too low. The supervisor argues that his ratings are generally low because his subordinates are generally inferior. 19.____
Of the following, the evidence MOST relevant to the point at issue can be secured by comparing efficiency ratings assigned by this supervisor

A. with ratings assigned by other supervisors in the same agency
B. this year with ratings assigned by him in previous years
C. to men recently transferred to his unit with ratings previously earned by these men
D. with the general city average of ratings assigned by all supervisors to all employees
E. with the relative order of merit of his employees as determined independently by promotion test marks

20. The one of the following which is NOT among the most common of the compensable factors used in wage evaluation studies is 20.____

A. initiative and ingenuity required
B. physical demand
C. responsibility for the safety of others
D. working conditions
E. presence of avoidable hazards

21. If independent functions are separated, there is an immediate gain in conserving special skills. If we are to make optimum use of the abilities of our employees, these skills must be conserved. 21.____
Assuming the correctness of this statement, it follows that

A. if we are not making optimum use of employee abilities, independent functions have not been separated
B. we are making optimum use of employee abilities if we conserve special skills
C. we are making optimum use of employee abilities if independent functions have been separated
D. we are not making optimum use of employee abilities if we do not conserve special skills
E. if special skills are being conserved, independent functions need not be separated

22. A reorganization of the bureau to provide for a stenographic pool instead of individual unit stenographers will result in more stenographic help being available to each unit when it is required, and consequently will result in greater productivity for each unit. An analysis of the space requirements shows that setting up a stenographic pool will require a minimum of 400 square feet of good space. In order to obtain this space, it will be necessary to reduce the space available for technical personnel, resulting in lesser productivity for each unit. 22.____
On the basis of the above discussion, it can be stated that in order to obtain greater productivity for each unit

A. a stenographic pool should be set up
B. further analysis of the space requirement should be made
C. it is not certain as to whether or not a stenographic pool should be set up
D. the space available for each technician should be increased in order to compensate for the absence of a stenographic pool
E. a stenographic pool should not be set up

23. The adoption of a single consolidated form will mean that most of the form will not be used in any one operation. This would create waste and confusion. 23.____
This conclusion is based upon the unstated hypothesis that

A. if waste and confusion are to be avoided, a single consolidated form should be used
B. if a single consolidated form is constructed, most of it can be used in each operation
C. if waste and confusion are to be avoided, most of the form employed should be used
D. most of a single consolidated form is not used
E. a single consolidated form should not be used

24. Assume that you are studying the results of mechanizing several hand operations. The type of data which would be MOST useful in proving that an increase in mechanization is followed by a lower cost of operation is data which show that in 24.____

A. some cases a lower cost of operation was not preceded by an increase in mechanization
B. no case was a higher cost of operation preceded by a decrease in mechanization
C. some cases a lower cost of operation was preceded by a decrease in mechanization
D. no case was a higher cost of operation preced by an increase in mechanization
E. some cases an increase in mechanization was followed by a decrease in cost of operation

25. The type of data which would be MOST useful in determining if an increase in the length of rest periods is followed by an increased rate of production is data which would indicate that 25.____

A. *decrease* in the total production never follows an increase in the length of the rest period
B. *increase* in the total production never follows an increase in the length of the rest period
C. *increase* in the rate of production never follows a decrease in the length of the rest period
D. *decrease* in the total production may follow a decrease in the length of the rest period
E. *increase* in the total production sometimes follows an increase in the length of the rest period

---

KEY (CORRECT ANSWERS)

1. E
2. B
3. C
4. B
5. E
6. A
7. B
8. A
9. A
10. D
11. C
12. C
13. B
14. D
15. E
16. B
17. E
18. E
19. C
20. E
21. D
22. C
23. C
24. D
25. A

TEST 3

DIRECTIONS: Each question or incomplete statement is followed by several suggested answers or completions. Select the one that BEST answers the question or completes the statement. *PRINT THE LETTER OF THE CORRECT ANSWER IN THE SPACE AT THE RIGHT.*

1. You have been asked to answer a request from a citizen of the city. After giving the request careful consideration you find that it cannot be granted. In answering the letter, you should begin by 1.____

   A. saying that the request cannot be granted
   B. discussing in detail the consideration you gave to the request
   C. quoting the laws relating to the request
   D. explaining in detail why the request cannot be granted
   E. indicating an alternative method of achieving the end desired

2. Reports submitted to the department head should be complete to the last detail. As far as possible, summaries should be avoided. This statement is, in general, 2.____

   A. *correct;* only on the basis of complete information can a proper decision be reached
   B. *incorrect;* if all reports submitted were of this character a department head would never complete his work
   C. *correct;* the decision as to what is important and what is not can only be made by the person who is responsible for the action
   D. *incorrect;* preliminary reports, obviously, cannot be complete to the last detail
   E. *correct;* summaries tend to conceal the actual state of affairs and to encourage generalizations which would not be made if the details were known; consequently they should be avoided if possible

3. The supervisor of a large bureau, who was required in the course of business to answer a large number of letters from the public, completely formalized his responses, that is, the form and vocabulary of every letter he prepared were the same as far as possible. This method of solving the problem of how to handle correspondence is, in general, 3.____

   A. *good;* it reduces the time and thought necessary for a response
   B. *bad;* the time required to develop a satisfactory standard form and vocabulary is usually not available in an active organization
   C. *good;* the use of standard forms causes similar requests to be answered in a similar way
   D. *bad;* the use of standard forms and vocabulary to the extent indicated results in letters in *officialese* hindering unambiguous explanation and clear understanding
   E. *good;* if this method were applied to an entire department, the answering of letters could be left to clerks and the administrators would be free for more constructive work

4. Of the following systems of designating the pages in a loose–leaf manual subject to constant revision and addition, the MOST practicable one is to use 4.____

   A. decimals for main divisions and integers for subdivisions
   B. integers for main divisions and letters for subdivisions
   C. integers for main divisions and decimals for subdivisions
   D. letters for main divisions and integers for subdivisions
   E. intergers for main divisions and integers for subdivisions

5. A subordinate submits a proposed draft of a form which is being revised to facilitate filling in the form on a typewriter. The draft shows that the captions for each space will be printed below the space to be filled in.
This proposal is 5.____

A. *undesirable;* it decreases visibility
B. *desirable;* it makes the form easy to understand
C. *undesirable;* it makes the form more difficult to understand
D. *desirable;* it increases visibility
E. *undesirable;* it is less compact than other layouts

6. The one of the following which is NOT an essential element of an integrated reporting system for work–measurement is a 6.____

A. uniform record form for accumulating data and instructions for its maintenance
B. procedure for routing reports upward through the organization and routing summaries downward
C. standard report form for summarizing basic records and instructions for its preparation
D. method for summarizing, analyzing and presenting data from several reports
E. looseleaf revisable manual which contains all procedural materials that are reasonably permanent and have a substantial reference value

7. Forms control only accomplishes the elimination, consolidation and simplifcation of forms. It constributes little to the elimination, consolidation and simplification of pro–cedures .
This statement is 7.____

A. *correct;* the form is static while the procedure is dynamic; consequently control of one does not necessarily result in control of the other
B. *incorrect;* forms frequently dictate the way work is laid out; consequently control of one frequently results in control of the other
C. *correct;* the procedure is primary and the form secondary; consequently control of procedure will also control form
D. *incorrect*; the form and procedure are identical from the viewpoint of work control; consequently control of one means control of the other
E. *correct;* the assurance that forms are produced and distributed economically has little relationship to the consolidation and simplification of procedures

8. Governmental agencies frequently attempt to avoid special interest group pressures by referring them to the predetermined legislative policy, or to the necessity for rules and regulations applying generally to all groups and situations.
Of the following, the MOST important weakness of this formally correct position is that 8.____

A. it is not tenable in the face of determined opposition
B. it tends to legalize and formalize the informal relationships between citizen groups and the government
C. the achievement of an agency's aims is in large measure dependent upon its ability to secure the cooperation and support of special interest groups
D. independent groups which participate in the formulation of policy in their sphere of interest tend to criticize openly and to press for changes in the direction of their policy
E. agencies following this policy find it difficult to decentralize their public relation activities as subdivisions can only refer to the agency's overall policy

9. One of the primary purposes of the performance budget is to improve the ability to examine budgetary requirement by groups who have not been engaged in the construction of the budget. This is acomplished by 9.____

   A. making line by line appropriations
   B. making lump sum appropriations by department
   C. enumerating authorization for all expenditures
   D. standardizing the language used and the kinds of authorizations permitted
   E. permitting examination on the level of accomplishment

10. When engaged in budget construction or budget analysis, there is no point in trying to determine the total or average benefits to be obtained from total expenditures for a particular commodity or function. 10.____
The validity of this argument is USUALLY based upon the

   A. viewpoint that it is not possible to construct a functional budget
   B. theory (or phenomenon) of diminishing utility
   C. hypothesis that as governmental budgets provide in theory for minimum requirements, there is no need to determine total benefits
   D. assumption that such determinations are not possible
   E. false hypothesis that a comparison between expected and achieved results does not aid in budget construction

Questions 11-12.

DIRECTIONS: Answer questions 11 and 12 on the basis of the following paragraph.

Production planning is mainly a process of synthesis. As a basis for the positive act of bringing complex production elements properly together, however, analysis is necessary, especially if improvement is to be made in an existing organization. The necessary analysis requires customary means of orientation and preliminary fact gathering with emphasis, however, on the recognition of administrative goals and of the relationship among work steps.

11. The entire process described is PRIMARILY one of 11.____

   A. taking apart, examining and recombining
   B. deciding what changes are necessary, making the changes and checking on their value
   C. fact finding so as to provide the necessary orientation
   D. discovering just where the emphasis in production should be placed and then modifying the existing procedure so that it is placed properly
   E. recognizing administrative goals and the relationship among work steps

12. In production planning according to the above paragraph, analysis is used PRIMARILY as 12.___

   A. a means of making important changes in an organization
   B. the customary means of orientation and preliminary fact finding
   C. a development of the relationship among work steps
   D. a means for holding the entire process intact by providing a logical basis
   E. a method to obtain the facts upon which a theory can be built

Questions 13-15.

DIRECTIONS: Answer questions 13 through 15 on the basis of the following paragraph.

Public administration is policy-making. But it is not autonomous, exclusive or isolated policy-making. It is policy–making on a field where mighty forces contend, forces engendered in and by society. It is policy-making subject to still other and various policy makers. Public administration is one of a number of basic political processes by which these people achieves and controls government.

13. From the point of view expressed in this paragraph, public administration is 13.___

   A. becoming a technical field with completely objective processes
   B. the primary force in modern society
   C. a technical field which should be divorced from the actual decision–making function
   D. basically anti–democratic
   E. intimately related to politics

14. According to the paragraph, public administration is NOT entirely 14.___

   A. a force generated in and by society
   B. subject at times to controlling influences
   C. a social process
   D. policy–making relating to administrative practices
   E. related to policy–making at lower levels

15. The paragraph asserts that public administration 15.___

   A. develops the basic and controlling policies
   B. is the result of policies made by many different forces
   C. should attempt to break through its isolated policy–making and engage on a broader field
   D. is a means of directing government
   E. is subject to the political processes by which acts are controlled

Questions 16–18.

DIRECTIONS: Answer questions 16 through 18 on the basis of the following paragraph.

In order to understand completely the source of an employee's insecurity on his job, it is necessary to understand how he came to be, who he is and what kind of a person he is away from his job. This would necessitate an understanding of those personal assets and liabilities which the employee brings to the job situation. These arise from his individual characteristics and his past experiences and established patterns of interpersonal relations. This whole area is of tremendous scope, encompassing everything included within the study of psychiatry and interpersonal relations. Therefore, it has been impracticable to consider it in detail. Attention has been focused on the relatively circumscribed area of the actual occupational situation. The factors considered those which the employee brings to the job situation and which arise from his individual characteristics and his past experience and established patterns of interpersonal relations are: intellectual–level or capacity, specific aptitudes, education, work experience, health, social and economic background, patterns of interpersonal relations and resultant personality characteristics.

16. According to the above paragraph, the one of the following I fields of study which would be of LEAST importance in the study of the problem is the 16.____

A. relationships existing among employees
B. causes of employee insecurity in the job situation
C. conflict, if it exists, between intellectual level and work experience
D. distribution of intellectual achievement
E. relationship between employee characteristics and the established pattern of interpersonal relations in the work situation

17. According to the above paragraph, in order to make a thoroughgoing and comprehensive study of the sources of employee insecurity, the field of study should include 17.____

A. only such circumscribed areas as are involved in extra–occupational situations
B. a study of the dominant mores of the period
C. all branches of the science of psychology
D. a determination of the characteristics, such as intellectual capacity, which an employee should bring to the job situation
E. employee personality characteristics arising from previous relationships with other people

18. It is implied by this paragraph that it would be of GREATEST advantage to bring to this problem a comprehensive knowledge of 18.____

A. all established patterns of interpersonal relations
B. the milieu in which the employee group is located
C. what assets and liabilities are presented in the job situation
D. methods of focusing attention on relatively circumscribed regions
E. the sources of an employee's insecurity on his job

Questions 19–20.

DIRECTIONS: Answer questions 19 and 20 on the basis of the following paragraph.

If, during a study, some hundreds of values of a variable (such as annual number of latenesses for each employee in a department) have been noted merely in the arbitrary order in which they happen to occur, the mind cannot properly grasp the significance of the record; the observations must be ranked or classified in some way before the characteristics of the series can be comprehended, and those comparisons, on which arguments as to causation depend, can be made with other series. A dichotomous classification is too crude; if the values are merely classified according to whether they exceed or fall short of some fixed value, a large part of the information given by the original record is lost. Numerical measurements lend themselves with peculiar readiness to a manifold classification.

19. According to the above statement, if the values of a variable which are gathered during a study are classified in a few subdivisions, the MOST likely result will be 19.____

A. an inability to grasp the significance of the record
B. an inability to relate the series with other series
C. a loss of much of the information in the original data
D. a loss of the readiness with which numerical measurements lend themselves to a manifold classification
E. that the order in which they happen to occur will be arbitrary

20. The above statement advocates, with respect to numerical data, the use of 20.____

A. arbitrary order
B. comparisons with other series
C. a two value classification
D. a many value classification
E. all values of a variable

Questions 21–25.

DIRECTIONS: Answer questions 21 trough 25 on the basis of the following chart.

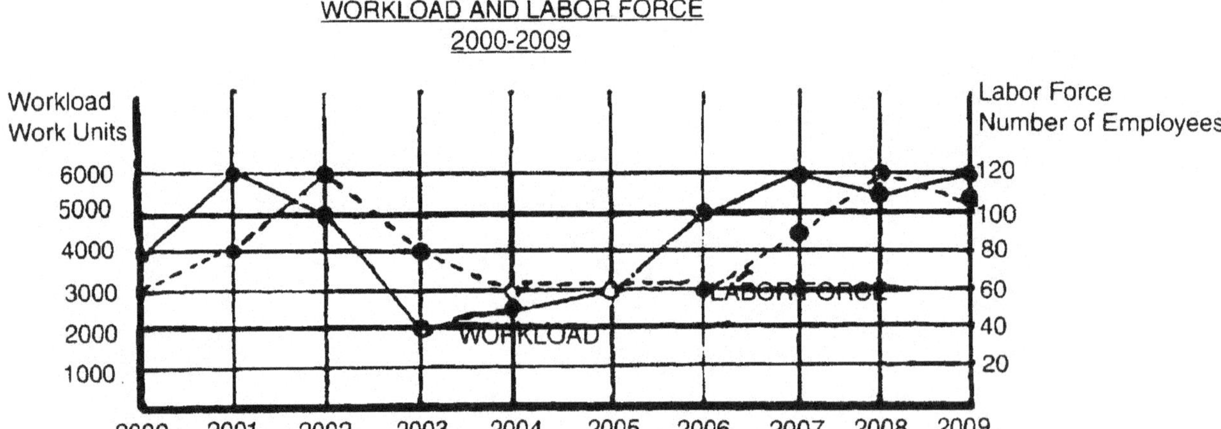

21. The one of the following years for which average employee production was LOWEST was 21.___

A. 2001 B. 2003 C. 2005 D. 2007 E. 2009

22. The average annual employee production for the ten–year period was, in terms of work units, MOST NEARLY 22.___

A. 30 B. 50 C. 70 D. 80 E. 90

23. On the basis of the chart, it can be deduced that personnel needs for the coming year are budgeted on the basis of 23.___

A. workload for the current year
B. expected workload for the coming year
C. no set plan
D. average workload over the five years immediately preceding the period
E. expected workload for the five coming years

24. The chart indicates that the operation is carefully programmed and that the labor force has been used properly.
This opinion is 24.___

A. *supported* by the chart; the organization has been able to meet emergency situations requiring much additional work without commensurate increases in staff
B. *not supported* by the chart; the irregular work load shows a complete absence of planning
C. *supported* by the chart; the similar shapes; of the workload and labor force curves show that these important factors are closely related
D. *not supported* by the chart; poor planning with respect to labor requirements is obvious from the chart
E. *supported* by the chart; the average number of units of work performed in any 5–year period during the 10 years shows sufficient regularity to indicate a definite trend

25. The chart indicates that the department may be organized in such a way as to require a permanent minimum staff which is too large for the type of operation indicated.
This opinion is 25.___

A. *supported* by the chart; there is indication that the operation calls for an irreducible minimum number of employees and application of the most favorable work production records show this to be too high for normal operation
B. *not supported* by the chart; the absence of any sort of regularity makes it impossible to express any opinion with any degree of certainty
C. *supported* by the chart; the expected close relationship between workload and labor force is displaced somewhat, a phenomenon which usually occurs as a result of a fixed minimum requirement
D. *not supported* by the chart; the violent movement of the labor force curve makes it evident that no minimum requirements are in effect
E. *supported* by the chart; calculation shows that the average number of employees was 84 with an average variation of 17.8, thus indicating that the minimum number of 60 persons was too high for efficient operation

KEY (CORRECT ANSWERS)

1. A
2. B
3. D
4. C
5. A

6. E
7. B
8. C
9. E
10. B

11. A
12. E
13. E
14. D
15. D

16. D
17. E
18. B
19. C
20. D

21. B
22. B
23. A
24. D
25. A

EXAMINATION SECTION
TEST 1

DIRECTIONS: Each question or incomplete statement is followed by several suggested answers or completions. Select the one that BEST answers the question or completes the statement. *PRINT THE LETTER OF THE CORRECT ANSWER IN THE SPACE AT THE RIGHT.*

1. The number of subordinates that can be supervised directly by one person tends to 1.____

   A. *increase* as the level of supervision progresses from the first-line supervisory level to the management level
   B. *decrease* as the duties of the subordinates increase in difficulty and complexity
   C. *decrease* with an increase in the knowledge and experience of the subordinates
   D. *increase* as the physical distance between supervisor and subordinates, as well as between the individual subordinates, increases

2. A study of the supervision of employees in an agency reveals that the bureau chiefs are reluctant to delegate responsibility and authority to their assistants. 2.____
   This study is *most likely* to reveal, in addition, that

   A. the organizational structure of this agency should be centralized
   B. the bureau chiefs tend to spend too much of their time on minor aspects of their work
   C. the number of employees supervised by bureau chiefs is excessive
   D. significant deviations from planned performance are not called to the attention of the bureau chiefs

3. The delegation of responsibility and authority to subordinates by their superior generally does NOT 3.____

   A. facilitate a division of labor or the development of specialization
   B. permit the superior to carry out programs of work that exceed his immediate personal limits of physical energy and knowledge
   C. result in a downward transfer of work, both mental and manual
   D. involve a transfer of ultimate responsibility from superior to subordinate

4. Horizontal coordination is achieved when the various units of a bureau work with mutual harmony and assistance. 4.____
   The achievement of such coordination is generally made *more difficult* when the chief of a large bureau

   A. conducts periodic conferences with supervisors of his operating units
   B. delegates some of his coordinating tasks to a staff assistant
   C. increases the number of specialized units in his bureau and the degree of their specialization
   D. transfers, subordinates from one to another of his operating units to broaden their understanding of the bureau's work

5. Some subdivision of work is imperative in large-scale operation. However, in subdividing work the superior should adopt the methods that have the greatest number of advantages and the fewest disadvantages. 5.____
The one of the following that is *most likely* to result from subdivision of work is

A. measuring work performed by employees is made more difficult
B. authority and responsibility for performance of particular operations are not clearly defined
C. standardizing work processes is made more difficult
D. work is delayed in passing between employees and between operating units

6. In developing a system for controlling the production of a bureau, the bureau chief should give consideration to reducing the fluctuations in the bureau's work load. 6.____
Of the following, the technique that is generally LEAST helpful in reducing fluctuations in work load is

A. staffing the bureau so that it can handle peak loads
B. maintaining a controlled backlog of work
C. regulating the timing of work routed to the bureau
D. changing the order of steps in work processes

7. The flow of work in an organization may be divided and channeled according to either a serial method or a parallel method. Under the serial method, the work moves through a single channel with each job progressing step by step through various work stations where a worker at each station completes a particular step of the job. Under the parallel method, the jobs are distributed among a number of workers, each worker completing all the steps of a job. The MOST accurate of the following statements regarding these two methods of dividing the flow of work is that 7.____

A. the training or break-in time necessary for workers to acquire processing skills is generally shorter under the parallel method
B. the serial method enables the workers to obtain a fuller understanding of the significance of their work
C. the parallel method tends to minimize the need for control devices to keep track of individual jobs in process
D. flexibility in the use of available staff is generally increased under the serial method

8. The executive who has immediate responsibility for a group of functions should have the right to decide what the structure of his organization shall be. 8.____
In making such decision, the executive should realize that

A. the lower the competence of a staff, the more important it is to maintain a sound organizational structure
B. the productivity of a competent staff will not be affected by an impairment in organizational structure
C. the productivity of a staff whose level of competency is low cannot be improved by an improvement in organizational structure
D. where there is a sound organizational structure there must of necessity be a sound organization

9. Of the following means that a bureau chief may utilize in training his understudy, the LEAST acceptable one is for him to 9.____

A. give the understudy assignments which other employees find too difficult or unpleasant
B. discuss with the understudy the important problems that confront the bureau chief
C. rotate the assignments given the understudy
D. give the understudy an opportunity to attend some of the meetings of bureau chiefs

10. Of the following practices and techniques that may be employed by the conference leader, the one that the conference leader should ordinarily AVOID is 10.____

A. permitting certain participants to leave the conference to get back to their work when the discussion has reached the point where their special interests or qualifications are no longer involved
B. encouraging the participants to take full written notes for later comparison with the minutes of the meeting
C. helping a participant extricate himself from an awkward position in which the participant has placed himself by an illadvised remark
D. translating the technical remarks of a speaker for the benefit of some participants who would otherwise fail to grasp the meaning of the remarks

11. In assigning work to his subordinates, a supervisor is MOST likely to lose the respect of his subordinates if he 11.____

A. reviews with a new employee the main points of an oral order issued to this employee
B. issues written orders instead of oral orders when a subordinate has repeatedly failed to carry out oral orders
C. gives oral orders regarding a task which the subordinate has performed satisfactorily in the past
D. gives an oral order which he feels the subordinate will not carry out

12. Both Agency X and Agency Y have district offices in all areas of the city. In Agency X the activities of the various districts are administered under centralized control, whereas in Agency Y the activities of the various district offices are administered under decentralized control. 12.____
The one of the following which is MORE characteristic of Agency X than of Agency Y is that in Agency X

A. activities of the district offices can more readily be adapted to meet the problems of the district served
B. there are greater opportunities for district administrators to develop resourcefulness
C. agency policies can be carried out with greater uniformity
D. decisions are made by individuals closer to the points at which problems arise

13. Of the following training methods, the one that is generally MOST valuable in teaching employees new clerical skills is 13.____

A. organized group discussion
B. individual instruction on the job
C. use of visual aids, such as charts and pictures
D. supervised reading, research and inspection

14. Department X maintains offices in each district of the city. Data gathered by the district offices are submitted monthly to the main office on a standard set of forms which are somewhat complicated.
Of the following methods of issuing detailed instructions for filing out the forms properly, the one generally considered MOST acceptable is 14.____

A. incorporating the instructions in the department's procedure manual
B. including an instructions sheet with each package of blank forms sent to a district office
C. printing the instructions on the back of each form
D. conducting periodic staff conferences devoted exclusively to discussions of the proper method of filling out the form

15. The one of the following which is usually LEAST affected by an increase in the personnel of an organization is the 15.____

A. problems of employee relationships
B. average amount of work performed by an employee
C. importance of coordinating the work of organizational units
D. number of first-line supervisors required

16. As part of his program to simplify clerical procedures, the chief of the records management division has decided to make an analysis of the forms used by his agency and to establish a system of forms control. He has assigned the assistant bureau chief to perform the bulk of the work in connection with this project. This assistant will receive part-time help from four subordinate employees.
Of the following actions the bureau chief may take in planning the work on this project, the MOST appropriate one is for him to 16.____

A. have the plans drawn up by the assistant and then submitted for final approval to the four part-time subordinates before work on the project is begun
B. have the assistant work with him in drawing up the plans and then present the plans to the four part-time subordinates for their comments
C. join with the five employees as a committee to formulate the plans for the project
D. prepare the plans himself and then submit the plans for approval to all five employees who are to work on the project

17. Bureau X is composed of several clerical units, each supervised by a unit head accountable to the bureau chief. Assume that the bureau chief has a special task for an employee of one of the clerical units and wishes to issue instructions directly to the employee regarding this task.
The LEAST appropriate of the following procedures for the bureau chief to follow is to 17.____

A. issue the instructions to the employee without notifying the employee's unit head
B. give the instructions to the employee in the presence of the unit head
C. ask the unit head to send the employee to him for instructions on this special task
D. tell the employee to inform his unit head of the bureau chief's instructions

18. A bureau chief has scheduled a conference with the unit heads in his bureau to obtain their views on a major problem confronting the bureau.
The LEAST appropriate action for him to take in conducting this conference is to 18.____

A. present his own views on the solution of the problem before asking the unit heads for their opinions
B. call upon a participant in the conference for information which this participant should have as part of his job
C. weigh the opinions expressed at the conference in the light of the individual speaker's background and experience
D. summarize briefly at the conclusion of the conference, the important points covered and the conclusions reached

19. Of the following, the greatest stress in selecting employees for office supervisory positions should ordinarily be placed on 19.____

A. intelligence and educational background
B. knowledge of the work and capacity for leadership
C. sincere interest in the activities and objectives of the agency
D. skill in performing the type of work to be supervised

20. The MOST acceptable of the following guides in preparing the specifications for a form is that 20.____

A. when forms are to be printed on colored paper, the dark shades of colored paper should be used
B. *tumble* or *head-to-foot* should be used if forms printed on both sides of the sheet are to be placed in binders with side binding
C. provision for ballot-type entries should be made if items requiring *yes* or *no* entries are to appear on the form
D. all-rag ledger paper rather than all-wood pulp bond paper should be used for forms which will receive little handling and will be kept for a short time

21. Suppose you are the chief of a bureau which contains several operating units. On one occasion you observe one of your unit heads severely reprimand a subordinate for violating a staff regulation. This subordinate has a good record for observing staff regulations, and you believe the severe reprimand will seriously undermine the morale of the employee. 21.____
Of the following, the BEST action for you to take in this situation is to

A. call both the unit head and the subordinate into your office at the same time and have each present his views on the matter to you
B. refrain from intervening in this matter because the unit head may resent any interference
C. take the subordinate aside, inform him that the unit head had not intended to reprimand him severely, and suggest that the matter be forgotten
D. discuss the matter with the unit head and suggest that he make some mitigating explanation to the subordinate

22. In addition to a report on its activities for the year, the one of the following items which it is MOST appropriate to include in an agency's annual report is 22.____

A. praise for each of the accomplishments of the agency during the year
B. pictures of agency personnel
C. history of the agency
D. descriptions of future activities and plans of the agency

23. Before transferring material from the active to the inactive files, the supervisor of the filing unit always consults the bureau heads directly concerned with the use of this material. This practice by the supervisor is 23.____

A. *desirable* chiefly because material that is no longer current for some bureaus may still be current for others
B. *undesirable* chiefly because it can only lead to disagreement among the bureau heads consulted
C. *desirable* chiefly because it is more economical to store records in transfer files than to keep them in the active files
D. *undesirable* chiefly because the filing supervisor is expected to make his own decision

24. The determination of essential factors in a specific kind of work and of qualifications of a worker necessary for its competent performance is MOST accurately defined as 24.____

A. job analysis
B. micro-motion study
C. cost analysis
D. production control

25. In the clinical approach to disciplinary problems, attention is focused on the basic causes of which the overt relations are merely symptomatic rather than on the specific violations which have brought the employee unfavorable notice. 25.____
The MOST accurate implication of this quotation is that the clinical approach

A. places emphasis on the actual violation rather than on the cause of the violation
B. attempts to promote greater insight into the underlying factors which have led to the infractions
C. does not evaluate the justness and utility of applying a specific penalty in a given situation
D. avoids the necessity for disciplinary action

26. The LEAST accurate of the following statements regarding the conduct of a conference is that 26.____

A. when there is great disparity in the rank of the participants at a conference, the conference leader should ordinarily refrain from requesting an opinion point blank from a participant of relatively low rank
B. when the aim of a conference is to obtain the opinion of a group of approxmately the same rank, the rank of the conference leader should ordinarily not be too much higher than that of the participants
C. in general, the chances that a conference will be fruitful are greatly increased if the conference leader's direct superior is one of the participants
D. a top administrator invited to present a brief talk sponsoring a series of conferences for line supervisors should generally arrange to leave the conference as soon as appropriate after he has made his speech

27. In preparing a report for release to the general public, the bureau chief should GENERALLY present at the beginning of the report 27.____

A. a description of the methods used in preparing the report
B. anticipated criticism of the report and the answer to this criticism
C. his conclusions and recommendations
D. a bibliography of the sources used in preparing the report

28. Staff or functional supervision in an organization 28.____

A. is least justified at the operational level
B. is contrary to the principle of Unity of Command
C. is more effective than authoritative supervision
D. normally does not give the right to take direct disciplinary action

29. Suppose that you are the supervisor of Clerical Unit A in a city agency. Work processed in your unit is sent to Clerical Unit B for further processing. One of your subordinates complains to you that the supervisor of Clerical Unit B has been offering him unwarranted criticism of the method in which his work is performed. 29.____
Of the following actions you may take, the MOST appropriate one for you to take FIRST is to

A. request the supervisor of Clerical Unit B to meet with you and your subordinate to discuss this matter
B. report this matter to this unit supervisor's immediate superior and request that this unsolicited criticism be discontinued
C. obtain the facts from the subordinate and then discuss the matter with this unit supervisor
D. tell your subordinate to refer the unit supervisor to you the next time he offers any criticism

30. This chart presents graphically a comparison of what is done and what is to be done. It is so ruled that each division of space represents both an amount of time and the quantity of work to be done during the particular unit of time. Horizontal lines drawn through these spaces show the relationship between the quantity of work actually done and that which is scheduled. 30.____
The chart referred to is known generally as a ______ chart.

A. progress or Gantt
B. job correlation
C. process or flow of work
D. Simo work simplification

31. The personnel survey is a systematic and reasonably exhaustive analysis and statement of the facts and forces in an organization which affect the relations between employees and management, and between employees and their work, followed by recommendations as to ways of developing better personnel policies and procedures. 31.____
On the basis of this statement, it is LEAST accurate to state that one of the purposes served by a personnel survey is to

A. appraise operating efficiency through an objective study of methods of production and a statistical interpretation of the facts
B. set forth items and causes of poor morale in an inclusive way and in their proper perspective
C. secure the facts to determine whether there is need of a more progressive personnel policy in an organization where personnel work is as yet undeveloped
D. evaluate the effectiveness of a personnel policy where a progressive personnel policy is already in operation

32. It is generally recognized that there is a relationship between the size of an organization's staff, the number of supervisory levels and the span of control (number of workers assigned to a supervisor). 32.____
The MOST accurate of the following statements regarding the relationship of these three elements is that

A. if the size of an organization's staff should remain unchanged and the span of control should increase, then the number of supervisory levels would tend to increase
B. if the size of the staff should decrease and the number of levels of supervision should increase, then the span of control would tend to decrease
C. if the size of the staff should increase and the number of supervisory levels should remain unchanged, then the span of control would tend to decrease
D. if the size of the staff should increase and the span of control should decrease, then the number of supervisory levels would tend to decrease

Questions 33-35.

DIRECTIONS: Questions 33 to 35 are to answered on the basis of the organization chart shown below. This chart presents the organizational structure of a division in a hypothetical agency. Each box designates a position in the organizational structure of this division. The symbol in each box represents the name of the individual occupying the position designated by the box. Thus, the name of the head of this division is represented by the symbol 1A.

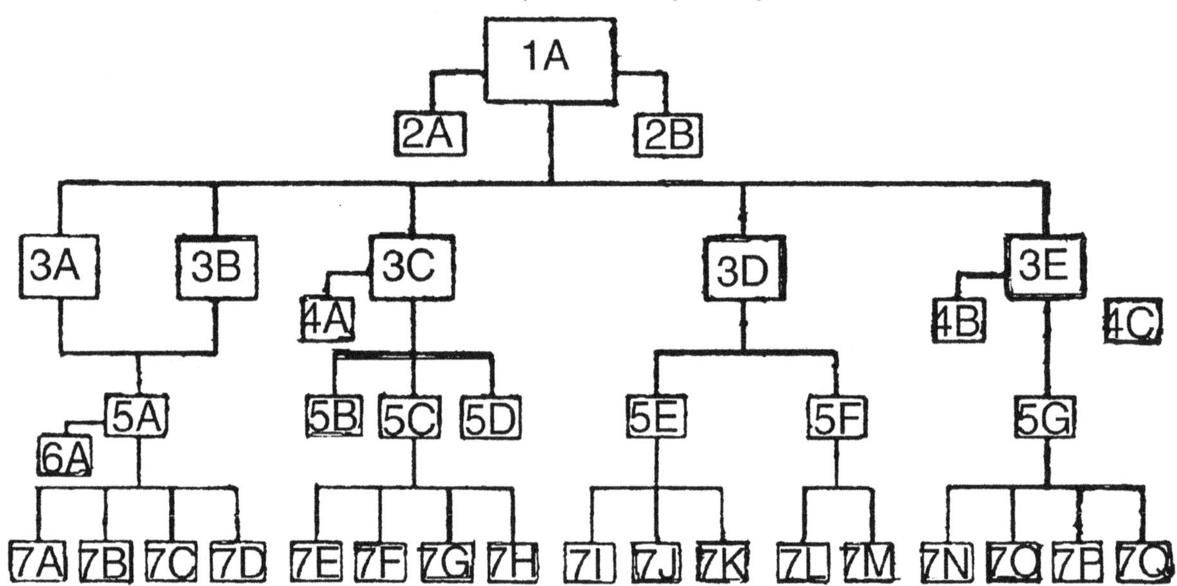

33. The one of the following who heads a subdivision which BEST illustrates in its organizational structure the characteristics of the pure line type of organization is 33.____

A. 3B B. 3C C. 3D D. 3E

34. The member of the organization who is MOST LIKELY to receive conflicting orders because he is directly accountable to more than one superior is 34.____

A. 5A B. 4A C. 5B D. 4C

35. Assume that 7K and 7P wish to exchange positions. Approval of this exchange must be obtained from each superior in the line of authority extending upward from 7K and from each superior in the line of authority extending upward from 7P. The one of the following who is NOT in a line of authority extending upward from either 7K or 7P is 35.____

A. 1A B. 3E C. 5F D. 3D

KEY (CORRECT ANSWERS)

1. B	11. D	21. D
2. B	12. C	22. D
3. D	13. B	23. A
4. C	14. A/C	24. A
5. D	15. B	25. B
6. A	16. B	26. C
7. C	17. A	27. C
8. A	18. A	28. D
9. A	19. B	29. C
10. B	20. C	30. A
	31. A	
	32. B	
	33. C	
	34. A	
	35. C	

TEST 2

DIRECTIONS: Each question or incomplete statement is followed by several suggested answers or completions. Select the one that BEST answers the question or completes the statement. *PRINT THE LETTER OF THE CORRECT ANSWER IN THE SPACE AT THE RIGHT.*

1. Analysis and simplification of office procedures are functions that should be conducted in all offices and on a continuing basis. These functions may be performed by the line supervisor, by staff methods specialists, or by outside consultants on methods analysis. An appraisal of these three methods of assigning responsibility for improving office procedures reveals that the LEAST accurate of the following statements is that 1.____

   A. outside consultants employed to simplify office procedures frequently bring with them a vast amount of previous experience as well as a fresh viewpoint
   B. line supervisors usually lack the special training which effective procedure analysis work requires
   C. continuity of effort and staff cooperation can better be secured by periodically employed consultants than by a permanent staff of methods analysts
   D. the reason line supervisors fail to keep procedures up to date is that the supervisor is too often overburdened with operating responsibilities

2. A man cannot serve two masters. 2.____
   This statement emphasizes MOST the importance in an organization of

   A. span of control
   B. specialization of work
   C. delegation of authority
   D. unity of command

3. An important aid in good office management is knowledge on the part of subordinates of the significance of their work. The possession of such knowledge by an employee will probably LEAST affect his 3.____

   A. interest in his work
   B. understanding of the relationship between the work of his unit and that of other units
   C. willingness to cooperate with other employees
   D. ability to undertake assignments requiring special skills

4. For mediocre executives who do not have a flair for positive administration, the implantation in subordinates of anxiety about job retention is a safe, if somewhat unimaginative, method of insuring a modicum of efficiency in the working organization. 4.____
   Of the following, the MOST accurate statement according to this quotation is that

   A. implanting anxiety about job retention is a method usually employed by the mediocre executive to improve the efficiency of his organization
   B. an organization will operate with at least some efficiency if employees realize that unsatisfactory work performance may subject them to dismissal
   C. successful executives with a flair for positive administration relieve their subordinates of any concern for their job security
   D. the implantation of anxiety about job security in subordinates should not be used as a method of improving efficiency

5. Savings of 20 per cent or more in clerical operating costs can often be achieved by improvement of the physical conditions under which office work is performed. In general, the MOST valid of the following statements regarding physical conditions is that 5.____

   A. conference rooms should have more light than small rooms
   B. the tops of desks should be glossy rather than dull
   C. noise is reflected more by hard-surfaced materials than by soft or porous materials
   D. yellow is a more desirable wall color for offices receiving an abundance of sunlight than for offices receiving little sunlight

6. To the executive who directs the complex and diverse operations of a large organizational unit, the conference is an important and, at times, indispensable tool of management. The inexperienced executive may, however, ploy the conference for a purpose for which it is ill fitted. Of the following, the LEAST use of the conference by the executive is to 6.____

   A. reconcile conflicting views or interests
   B. develop an understanding by all concerned of a policy already adopted
   C. coordinate an activity involving several line supervisors
   D. perform technical research on a specific project

7. In planning the layout of office space, the office supervisor should bear in mind that one large room is a more efficient operating unit than the same number of square feet split up into smaller rooms. Of the following, the LEAST valid basis for the preceding statement is that in the large room 7.____

   A. better light and ventilation are possible
   B. flow of work between employees is more direct
   C. supervision and control are more easily maintained
   D. time and motion studies are easier to conduct

8. The one of the following companies which is BEST known as a manufacturer of filing cabinets and office furniture is 8.____

   A. Pitney-Bowes, Inc.
   B. Dennison Manufacturing Co.
   C. Wilson-Jones Co.
   D. Shaw-Walker Co.

9. The program used to deliver audio-visual office presentations is known as 9.____

   A. PowerPoint
   B. Excel
   C. CGI
   D. Dreamweaver

10. The principles of scientific office management are MOST FREQUENTLY applied by government office supervisors in 10.____

   A. maintaining flexibility in hiring and firing
   B. developing improved pay scales
   C. standardizing clerical practices and procedures
   D. revising organizational structure

11. The one of the following factors to which the bureau head should attach LEAST importance in deciding on the advisability of substituting machine for manual operations in a given area of office work is the 11.____

    A. need for accuracy in the work
    B. relative importance of the work
    C. speed with which the work must be completed
    D. volume of work

12. The clerk displayed a *rudimentary* knowledge of the principles of supervision. 12.____
    The word *rudimentary* as used in this sentence means MOST NEARLY

    A. thorough B. elementary C. surprising D. commendable

13. This is an *integral* part of our program. 13.____
    The word *integral* as used in this sentence means MOST NEARLY

    A. minor B. unknown C. essential D. well-developed

14. A *contiguous* office is one that is 14.____

    A. spacious B. rectangular in shape
    C. adjoining D. crowded

15. This program was *sanctioned* by the department head. 15.____
    The word *sanctioned* as used in this sentence means MOST NEARLY

    A. devised B. approved C. modified D. rejected

16. The file clerk performed his work in a *perfunctory* manner. 16.____
    The word *perfunctory* as used in this sentence means MOST NEARLY

    A. quiet B. orderly C. sullen D. indifferent

17. He did not *impugn* the reasons given for the change in policy. 17.____
    The word *impugn* as used in this sentence means MOST NEARLY

    A. make insinuations against B. verify in whole or part
    C. volunteer support for D. overlook or ignore

18. The supervisor was unable to learn the identity of the *culpable* employee. 18.____
    The word *culpable* as used in this sentence means MOST NEARLY

    A. inaccurate B. careless C. guilty D. dishonest

19. The announcement was made at a *propitious* time. 19.____
    The word *propitious* as used in this sentence means MOST NEARLY

    A. unexpected B. busy C. favorable D. significant

20. He showed no *compunction* in carrying out this order. 20.____
    The word *compunction* as used in this sentence means MOST NEARLY

    A. feeling of remorse B. hesitation or delay
    C. tact or discretion D. disposition to please

21. He acted in a *fiduciary* capacity. 21.____
The word *fiduciary* as used in this sentence means MOST NEARLY

A. administrative or executive in nature
B. quasi-legal in nature
C. involving confidence or trust
D. requiring auditing or budgetary ability

22. To *temporize* means MOST NEARLY to 22.____

A. allay temporarily the fears of
B. render a temporary service
C. yield temporarily to prevailing opinion
D. react temperamentally

23. The new supervisor was *sanguine* about the prospects of success. 23.____
The word *sanguine* as used in this sentence means MOST NEARLY

A. uncertain B. confident C. pessimistic D. excited

24. The supervisor was asked to *implement* the new policy. 24.____
The word *implement* as used in this sentence means MOST NEARLY

A. explain B. revise C. delay the announcement of
D. carry into effect

25. The word *intimation* means MOST NEARLY 25.____

A. friendliness B. an attempt to frighten
C. a difficult task D. an indirect suggestion

26. Mr. Jones has a *penchant* for this type of work. 26.____
The word *penchant* as used in this sentence means MOST NEARLY

A. record of achievement B. unexplainable dislike
C. lack of aptitude D. strong inclination

27. The speaker's comments were *desultory*. 27.____
The word *desultory* as used in this sentence means MOST NEARLY

A. inspiring B. aimless C. pertinent D. rude

Questions 28-35.

DIRECTIONS: Questions 28 through 35 are to be answered SOLELY on the basis of the following chart which relates to the Investigation Division of Dept. X. This chart contains four curves which connect the points that show for each year the variations in percentage deviation from normal in the number of investigators, the number of clerical employees, the cost of personnel, and the number of cases processed for the period 2002-2012 inclusive. The year 2002 was designated as the normal year. The personnel of the Investigation Division consists of investigators and clerical employees only.

INVESTIGATION DIVISION, DEPARTMENT X

VARIATIONS IN NUMBER OF CASES PROCESSED, COST OF PERSONNEL. NUMBER OF CLERICAL EMPLOYEES, AND NUMBER OF INVESTIGATORS FOR EACH YEAR FROM 2002 to 2012 INCLUSIVE
(In percentages from normal)

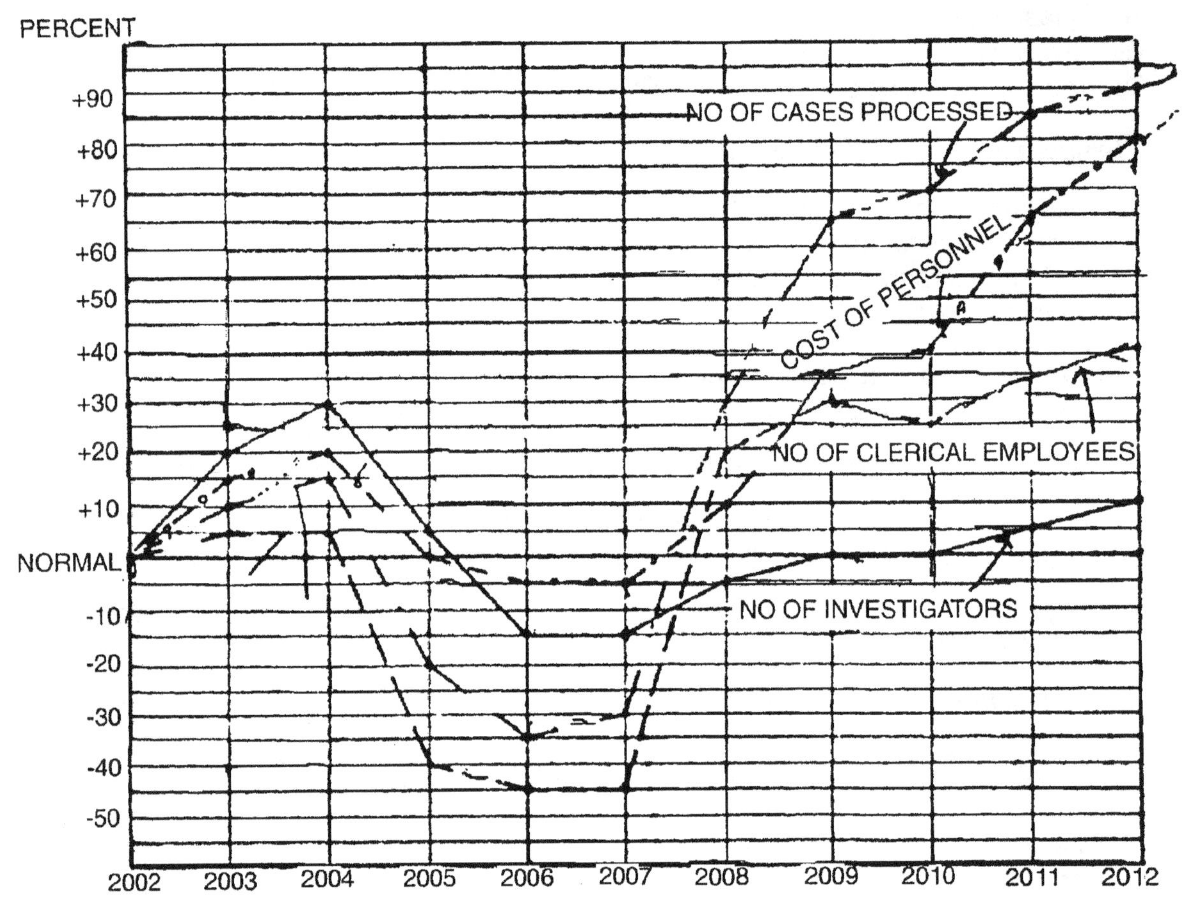

Example: If there were 80 clerical employees in the division in 1992, then the number of clerical employees in the division in 1999 was 104.

28. If 1300 cases were processed by the division in 2006, then the number of cases processed in 2002 was 28.____

A. 2000 B. 1755 C. 2145 D. 1650

29. Of the following, the year in which there was no change in the size of the division's total staff from that of the preceding year is 29.____

A. 2005 B. 2006 C. 2009 D. 2011

30. Of the following, the year in which the size of the division's staff *decreased* MOST sharply from that of the preceding year is 30.____

A. 2005 B. 2006 C. 2007 D. 2008

31. An inspection of the chart discloses that the curve that fluctuates *least* as determined by the average deviation from normal, is the curve for the 31.____

A. number of cases processed
B. cost of personnel
C. number of clerical employees
D. number of investigators

32. A comparison of 2006 with 2012 reveals an increase in 2006 in the 32.____

A. cost of personnel for the division
B. number of cases processed per investigator
C. number of cases processed per clerical employee
D. number of clerical employees per investigator

33. If the personnel cost per case processed in 2002 was $12.30, then the personnel cost per case processed in 2012 was MOST NEARLY 33.____

A. $9.85 B. $10.95 C. $11.65 D. $13.85

34. Suppose that there was a total of 108 employees in the division in 2002 and a total of 125 employees in 2010. 34.____
On the basis of these figures, it is MOST accurate to state that the number of investigators employed in the division in 2010 was

A. 40 B. 57 C. 68 D. 85

35. It is predicted that the number of cases processed in 2013 will exceed the number processed in 2002 by exactly the same quantity that the number processed in 2012 exceeded that processed in 2011. It is also predicted that the personnel cost in 2013 will exceed the personnel cost in 2012 by exactly the same amount that the 2012 personnel cost exceeded that for 2011. On the basis of these predictions, it is MOST accurate to state that the personnel cost per case in 2013 will be 35.____

A. ten per cent less than the personnel cost per case in 2012
B. exactly the same as the personnel cost per case in 2012
C. twice as much as the personnel cost per case in 2002
D. exactly the same as the personnel cost per case in 2002

KEY (CORRECT ANSWERS)

1. C
2. D
3. D
4. B
5. C

6. D
7. D
8. D
9. A
10. C

11. B
12. B
13. C
14. C
15. B

16. D
17. A
18. C
19. C
20. A

21. C
22. C
23. B
24. D
25. B

26. D
27. B
28. A
29. B
30. A

31. D
32. C
33. C
34. A
35. D

SUPERVISION, ADMINISTRATION, MANAGEMENT AND ORGANIZATION

EXAMINATION SECTION
TEST 1

DIRECTIONS: Each question or incomplete statement is followed by several suggested answers or completions. Select the one that BEST answers the question or completes the statement. *PRINT THE LETTER OF THE CORRECT ANSWER IN THE SPACE AT THE RIGHT.*

1. In coaching a subordinate on the nature of decision–making, an executive would be right if he stated that the one of the following which is *generally* the BEST definition of decision-making is: 1.____

   A. Choosing between alternatives
   B. Making diagnoses of feasible ends
   C. Making diagnoses of feasible means
   D. Comparing alternatives

2. Of the following, which one would be LEAST valid as a purpose of an organizational policy statement? To 2.____

   A. keep personnel from performing improper actions and functions on routine matters
   B. prevent the mishandling of non-routine matters
   C. provide management personnel with a tool that precludes the need for their use of judgment
   D. provide standard decisions and approaches in handling problems of a recurrent nature

3. Much has been written criticizing bureaucratic organizations. Current thinking on the subject is GENERALLY that 3.____

   A. bureaucracy is on the way out
   B. bureaucracy, though not perfect, is unlikely to be replaced
   C. bureaucratic organizations are most effective in dealing with constant change
   D. bureaucratic organizations are most effective when dealing with sophisticated customers or clients

4. The development of alternate plans as a major step in planning will normally result in the planner having several possible courses of action available. GENERALLY, this is 4.____

   A. *desirable,* since such development helps to determine the most suitable alternative and to provide for the unexpected
   B. *desirable,* since such development makes the use of planning premises and constraints unnecessary
   C. *undesirable,* since the planners should formulate only one way of achieving given goals at a given time
   D. *undesirable,* since such action restricts efforts to modify the planning to take advantage of opportunities

5. The technique of departmentation by task force includes the assigning of a team or task force to a definite project or block of work which extends from the beginning to the completing of a wanted and definite type and quantity of work. Of the following, the MOST important factor aiding the successful use of this technique *normally* is 5.____

   A. having the task force relatively large, at least one hundred members
   B. having a definite project termination date established
   C. telling each task force member what his next assignment will be only after the current project ends
   D. utilizing it only for projects that are regularly recurring

6. With respect to communication in small group settings such as may occur in business, government and the military, it is GENERALLY true that people *usually* derive more satisfaction and are usually more productive under conditions which 6.____

   A. permit communication only with superiors
   B. permit the minimum intragroup communication possible
   C. are generally restricted by management
   D. allow open communication among all group members

7. If an executive were asked to list some outstanding features of decentralization, which one of the following would NOT be such a feature? Decentralization 7.____

   A. provides decision-making experience for lower level managers
   B. promotes uniformity of policy
   C. is a relatively new concept in management
   D. is similar to the belief in encouragement of free enterprise

8. Modern management experts have emphasized the importance of the informal organization in motivating employees to increase productivity. Of the following, the characteristic which would have the MOST direct influence on employee motivation is the tendency of members of the informal organization to 8.____

   A. resist change
   B. establish their own norms
   C. have similar outside interests
   D. set substantially higher goals than those of management

9. According to leading management experts, the decision-making process contains separate and distinct steps that must be taken in an orderly sequence. Of the following arrangements, which one is in CORRECT order? 9.____

   A. I. Search for alternatives II.diagnosis III. comparison IV. choice
   B. I.Diagnosis II. comparison III. search for alternatives IV. choice
   C. I. Diagnosis II. search for alternatives III. comparison IV. choice
   D. I.Diagnosis II.search for alternatives III. choice IV. comparison

10. Of the following, the growth of professionalism in large organizations can PRIMARILY be expected to result in 10.____

   A. greater equalization of power
   B. increased authoritarianism
   C. greater organizational disloyalty
   D. increased promotion opportunities

11. Assume an executive carries out his responsibilities to his staff according to what is now known about managerial leadership. Which of the following statements would MOST accurately reflect his assumptions about proper management? 11.____

   A. Efficiency in operations results from allowing the human element to participate in a minimal way.
   B. Efficient operation results from balancing work considerations with personnel considerations.
   C. Efficient operation results from a workforce committed to its self interest.
   D. Efficient operation results from staff relationships that produce a friendly work climate.

12. Assume that an executive is called upon to conduct a management audit. To do this properly, he would have to take certain steps in a specific sequence. Of the following steps, which step should this manager take FIRST? 12.____

   A. Managerial performance must be surveyed.
   B. A method of reporting must be established.
   C. Management auditing procedures and documentation must be developed.
   D. Criteria for the audit must be considered.

13. If a manager is required to conduct a scientific investigation of an organizational problem, the FIRST step he should take is to 13.____

   A. state his assumptions about the problem
   B. carry out a search for background information
   C. choose the right approach to investigate the validity of his assumptions
   D. define and state the problem

14. An executive would be *right* to assert that the principle of delegation states that decisions should be made PRIMARILY 14.____

   A. by persons in an executive capacity qualified to make them
   B. by persons in a non-executive capacity
   C. at as low an organization level of authority as practicable
   D. by the next lower level of authority

15. Of the following, which one is NOT regarded by management authorities as a FUNDAMENTAL characteristic of an *ideal* bureaucracy? 15.____

   A. Division of labor and specialization
   B. An established hierarchy
   C. Decentralization of authority
   D. A set of operating rules and regulations

16. As the number of subordinates in a manager's span of control increases, the ACTUAL number of possible relationships 16.____

   A. increases disproportionately to the number of subordinates
   B. increases in equal number to the number of subordinates
   C. reaches a stable level
   D. will first increase then slowly decrease

17. An executive's approach to controlling the activities of his subordinates concentrated on ends rather than means, and was diagnostic rather than punitive. This manager may MOST properly be characterized as using the managerial technique of management-by- 17.____

A. exception B. objectives C. crisis D. default

18. In conducting a training session on the administrative control process, which of the following statements would be LEAST calid for an executive to make? Controlling 18.____

A. requires checking upon assignments to see what is being done
B. involves comparing what is being done to what ought to be done
C. requires corrective action when what is being done does not meet expectations
D. occurs after all the other managerial processes have been performed

19. The "brainstorming" technique for creative solutions of management problems MOST generally consists of 19.____

A. bringing staff together in an exchange of a quantity of free wheeling ideas
B. isolating individual staff members to encourage thought
C. developing improved office procedures
D. preparation of written reports on complex problems

20. Computer systems hardware MOST often operates in relation to which one of the following steps in solving a data-processing problem? 20.____

A. Determining the problem
B. Defining and stating the problem
C. Implementing the programmed solution
D. Completing the documentation of every unexplored solution

21. There is a tendency in management to upgrade objectives. This trend is generally regarded as 21.____

A. *desirable;* the urge to improve is demonstrated by adopting objectives that have been adjusted to provide improved service
B. *undesirable;* the typical manager searches for problems which obstruct his objectives
C. *desirable;* it is common for a manager to find that the details of an immediate operation have occupied so much of his time that he has lost sight of the basic overall objective
D. *undesirable;* efforts are wasted when they are expended on a mass of uncertain objectives, since the primary need of most organizations is a single target or several major ones

22. Of the following, it is generally LEAST effective for an executive to delegate authority where working conditions involve 22.____

A. rules establishing normal operating procedures
B. consistent methods of operation
C. rapidly changing work standards
D. complex technology

23. If an executive was explaining the difficulty of making decisions under *risk* conditions, he would be MOST accurate if he said that such decisions would be difficult to make when the decision maker has 23.____

A. limited information and experience and can expect many outcomes for each action
B. much information and experience and can expect many outcomes for each action
C. much information and experience and can expect few outcomes for each action
D. limited information and experience and can expect few outcomes for each action

24. If an executive were asked to list some outstanding features of centralized organization, which one of the following would be INCORRECT? Centralized organization 24.____

A. lessens risks of errors by unskilled subordinates
B. utilizes the skills of specialized experts at a central location
C. produces uniformity of policy and non-uniformity of action
D. enables closer control of operations than a decentralized set-up

25. It is possible for an organization's management to test whether or not the organization has a sound structure. Of the following, which one is NOT a test of soundness in an organization's structure? The 25.____

A. ability to replace key personnel with minimum loss of effectiveness
B. ability of information and decisions to flow more freely through the *grapevine* than through formal channels
C. presence of definite objectives for each unit in the organizational system
D. provision for orderly organizational growth with the ability to handle change as the need arises

---

KEY(CORRECT ANSWERS)

1. A
2. C
3. B
4. A
5. B
6. D
7. B
8. B
9. C
10. A
11. B
12. D
13. D
14. C
15. C
16. A
17. B
18. D
19. A
20. C
21. A
22. C
23. A
24. C
25. B

TEST 2

DIRECTIONS: Each question or incomplete statement is followed by several suggested answers or completions. Select the one that BEST answers the question or completes the statement. *PRINT THE LETTER OF THE CORRECT ANSWER IN THE SPACE AT THE RIGHT.*

1. Management experts generally believe that computer-based management information systems (MIS) have greater potential for improving the process of management than any other development in recent decades. The one of the following which MOST accurately describes the objectives of MIS is to 1.____

   A. provide information for decision-making on planning, initiating, and controlling the operations of the various units of the organization
   B. establish mechanization of routine functions such as clerical records, payroll, inventory and accounts receivable in order to promote economy and efficiency
   C. computerize decision-making on planning, initiative, organizing and controlling the operations of an organization
   D. provide accurate facts and figures on the various programs of the organization to be used for purposes of planing and research

2. The one of the following which is the BEST application on the *management-by-exception* principle is that this principle 2.____

   A. stimulates communication and aids in management of crisis situations, thus reducing the frequency of decision-making
   B. saves time and reserves top-management decisions only for crisis situations, thus reducing the frequency of decision-making
   C. stimulates communication, saves time and reduces the frequency of decision-making
   D. is limited to crisis-management situations

3. It is *generally* recognized that each organization is dependent upon the availability of qualified personnel. Of the following, the MOST important factor affecting the availability of qualified people to each organization is 3.____

   A. innovations in technology and science
   B. the general decline in the educational levels of our population
   C. the rise of sentiment against racial discrimination
   D. pressure by organized community groups

4. A *fundamental* responsibility of all managers is to decide what physical facilities and equipment are needed to help attain basic goals. Good planning for the purchase and use of equipment is seldom easy to do and is *complicated* MOST by the fact that 4.____

   A. organizations rarely have stable sources of supply
   B. nearly all managers tend to be better at personnel planning than at equipment planning
   C. decisions concerning physical resources are made too often on a *crash basis* rather than under carefully prepared policies
   D. legal rulings relative to depreciation fluctuate very frequently

5. In attempting to reconcile managerial objectives and an individual employee's goals, it is generally LEAST desirable for management to 5.____

   A. recognize the capacity of the individual to contribute toward realization of managerial goals
   B. encourage self-development of the employee to exceed minimum job performance
   C. consider an individual employee's work separately from other employees
   D. demonstrate that an employee advances only to the extent that he contributes directly to the accomplishment of stated goals

6. As a management tool for discovering individual training needs a job analysis would generally be of LEAST assistance in determining 6.____

   A. the performance requirements of individual jobs
   B. actual employee performance on the job
   C. acceptable standards of performance
   D. training needs for individual jobs

7. One of the major concerns of organizational managers today is how the spread of automation will affect them and the status of their positions. Realistically speaking, one can say that the MOST likely effect of our newer forms of highly automated technology on managers will be to 7.____

   A. make most top-level positions superfluous or obsolete
   B. reduce the importance of managerial work in general
   C. replace the work of managers with the work of technicians
   D. increase the importance of and demand for top managerial personnel

8. Which one of the following is LEAST likely to be an area or cause of trouble in the use of staff people (e.g., assistants to the administrator)? 8.____

   A. Misunderstanding of the role the staff people are supposed to play, as a result of vagueness of definition of their duties and authority
   B. Tendency of staff personnel almost always to be older than line personnel at comparable salary levels with whom they must deal
   C. Selection of staff personnel who fail to have simultaneously both competence in their specialties and skill in staff work
   D. The staff person fails to understand mixed staff and operating duties

9. The one of the following which is the BEST measure of decentralization in an agency is the 9.____

   A. amount of checking required on decisions made at lower levels in the chain of command
   B. amount of checking required on decisions made at lower levels of the chain of command and the number of functions affected thereby
   C. number of functions affected by decisions made at higher levels
   D. number of functions affected by middle echelon decision-making

10. Which of the following is generally NOT a valid statement with respect to the supervisory process? 10.____

A. General supervision is more effective than close supervision.
B. Employee-centered supervisors lead more effectively than do production-centered supervisors.
C. Employee satisfaction is directly related to productivity.
D. Low-producing supervisors use techniques that are different from high-producing supervisors

11. The one of the following which is the MOST essential element for proper evaluation of the performance of subordinate supervisors is a 11.____

A. careful definition of each supervisor's specific job responsibilities and of his progress in meeting mutually agreed upon work goals
B. system of rewards and penalties based on each supervisor's progress in meeting clearly defined performance standards
C. definition of personality traits, such as industry, initiative, dependability and cooperativeness, required for effective job performance
D. breakdown of each supervisor's job into separate components and a rating of his performance on each individual task

12. The one of the following which is the PRINCIPAL advantage of specialization for the operating efficiency of a public service agency is that specialization 12.____

A. reduces the amount of red tape in coordinating the activities of mutually dependent departments
B. simplifies the problem of developing adequate job controls
C. provides employees with a clear understanding of the relationship of their activities to the overall objectives of the agency
D. reduces destructive competition for power between departments

13. Of the following, the group which *generally* benefits MOST from supervisory training programs in public service agencies are those supervisors who have 13.____

A. accumulated a long period of total service to the agency
B. responsibility for a large number of subordinate personnel
C. been in the supervisory ranks for a long period of time
D. a high level of formalized academic training

14. A list of conditions which encourages good morale inside a work group would NOT include a 14.____

A. high rate of agreement among group members on values and objectives
B. tight control system to minimize the risk of individual error
C. good possibility that joint action will accomplish goals
D. past history of successful group accomplishment

15. Of the following, the MOST important factor to be considered in selecting a training strategy or program is the 15.____

A. requirements of the job to be performed by the trainees
B. educational level or prior training of the trainees
C. size of the training group
D. quality and competence of available training specialists

16. Of the following, the one which is considered to be LEAST characteristic of the higher ranks of management is 16.____

    A. that higher levels of management benefit from modern technology
    B. that success is measured by the extent to which objectives are achieved
    C. the number of subordinates that directly report to an executive
    D. the deemphasis of individual and specialized performance

17. Assume that an executive is preparing a training syllabus to be used in training members of his staff. Which of the following would NOT be a valid principle of the learning process for this manager to keep in mind in the preparation of the training syllabus? 17.____

    A. When a person has thoroughly learned a task, it takes a lot of effort to create a little more improvement
    B. In complicated learning situations, there is a period in which an additional period of practice produces an equal amount of improvement in learning
    C. The less a person knows about the task, the slower the initial progress
    D. The more the person knows about the task, the slower the initial progress

18. Of the following, which statement BEST illustrates when collective bargaining agreements are working well? 18.____

    A. Executives strongly support subordinate managers.
    B. The management rights clause in the contract is clear and enforced.
    C. Contract provisions are competently interpreted.
    D. The provisions of the agrement are properly interpreted, communicated and observed.

19. An executive who wishes to encourage subordinates to communicate freely with him about a job-related problem should FIRST 19.____

    A. state his own position on the problem before listening to the subordinates' ideas
    B. invite subordinates to give their own opinions on the problem
    C. ask subordinates for their reactions to his own ideas about the problem
    D. guard the confidentiality of management information about the problem

20. The ability to deal constructively with intra-organizational conflict is an essential attribute of the successful manager. The one of the following types of conflict which would be LEAST difficult to handle constructively is a situation in which there is 20.____

    A. agreement on objectives, but disagreement as to the probable results of adopting the various alternatives
    B. agreement on objectives, disagreement on alternative courses of action, and relative certainty as to the outcome of one of the alternatives
    C. disagreement on objectives and on alternative courses of action, but relative certainty as to the outcome of the alternatives
    D. disagreement on objectives and on alternative courses of action, but uncertainty as to the outcome of the alternatives

21. Which of the following statements is LEAST accurate in describing formal job evaluation and wage and salary classification plans? 21.____

    A. Parties that disagree on wage matters can examine an established system rather than unsupported opinions.
    B. The use of such plans tends to overlook the effect of age and seniority of employees on job values in the plan
    C. Such plans can eliminate salary controversies in organizations designing and using them properly
    D. These plans are not particularly useful in checking on executive compensation

22. In carrying out disciplinary action, the MOST important procedure for all managers to follow is to 22.____

    A. sell all levels of management on the need for discipline from the organization's viewpoint
    B. follow up on a disciplinary action and not assume that the action has been effective
    C. convince all executives that proper discipline is a legitimate tool for their use
    D. convince all executives that they need to display confidence in the organization's rules

Questions 23–25.

DIRECTIONS: Questions 23 through 25 are based on the following situation. Richard Ford, a top administrator, is responsible for output in his organization. Because productivity had been lagging for two periods in a row, Ford decided to establish a committee of his subordinate managers to investigate the reasons for the poor performance and to make recommendations for improvements. After two meetings, the committee came to the conclusions and made the recommendations that follow:

Output forecasts had been handed down from the top without prior consultation with middle management and first level supervision. Lines of authority and responsibility had been unclear. The planning and control process should be decentralized.

After receiving the committee's recommendations, Ford proceeded to take the following actions:

Ford decided he would retain final authority to establish quotas but would delegate to the middle managers the responsibility for meeting quotas.

After receiving Ford's decision, the middle managers proceeded to delegate to the first-line supervisors the authority to establish their own quotas. The middle managers eventually received and combined the first-line supervisors' quotas so that these conformed with Ford's.

23. Ford's decision to delegate responsibility for meeting quotas to the middle managers is INCONSISTENT with sound management principles because of which one of the following? 23.____

    A. Ford shouldn't have involved himself in the first place.
    B. Middle managers do not have the necessary skills.
    C. Quotas should be established by the chief executive.
    D. Responsibility should not be delegated.

24. The principle of coextensiveness of responsibility and authority bears on Ford's decision. In this case, it IMPLIES that 24.____

A. authority should exceed responsibility
B. authority should be delegated to match the degree of responsibility
C. both authority and responsibility should be retained and not delegated
D. responsibility should be delegated but authority should be retained

25. The middle managers' decision to delegate to the first-line supervisors the authority to establish quotas was INCORRECTLY reasoned because 25.____

A. delegation and control must go together
B. first-line supervisors are in no position to establish quotas
C. one cannot delegate authority that one does not possess
D. the meeting of quotas should not be delegated

KEY(CORRECT ANSWERS)

1. A
2. C
3. A
4. C
5. C
6. B
7. D
8. B
9. B
10. C
11. A
12. B
13. D
14. B
15. A
16. C
17. D
18. D
19. B
20. B
21. C
22. B
23. D
24. B
25. C

TEST 3

DIRECTIONS: Each question or incomplete statement is followed by several suggested answers or completions. Select the one that BEST answers the question or completes the statement. *PRINT THE LETTER OF THE CORRECT ANSWER IN THE SPACE AT THE RIGHT.*

1. A danger which exists in any organization as complex as that required for administration of a large public agency, is that each department comes to believe that it exists for its own sake.The one of the following which has been attempted in some organizations as a cure for this condition is to 1.____

   A. build up the departmental esprit de corps
   B. expand the functions and jurisdictions of the various departments so that better integration is possible
   C. develop a body of specialists in the various subject matter fields which cut across departmental lines
   D. delegate authority to the lowest possible echelon
   E. systematically transfer administrative personnel from one department to another

2. At best, the organization chart is ordinarily and necessarily an idealized picture of the intent of top management, a reflection of hopes and aims rather than a photograph of the operating facts within the organization. 2.____
   The one of the following which is the basic reason for this is that the organization chart

   A. does not show the flow of work within the organization
   B. speaks in terms of positions rather than of live employees
   C. frequently contains unresolved internal ambiguities
   D. is a record of past organization or of proposed future organization and never a photograph of the living organization
   E. does not label the jurisdiction assigned to each component unit

3. The drag of inadequacy is always downward. The need in administration is always for the reverse; for a department head to project his thinking to the city level, for the unit chief to try to see the problems of the department. 3.____
   The inability of a city administration to recruit administrators who can satisfy this need usually results in departments characterized by

   A. disorganization
   B. poor supervision
   C. circumscribed viewpoints
   D. poor public relations
   E. a lack of programs

4. When, as a result of a shift in public sentiment, the elective officers of a city are changed, is it desirable for career administrators to shift ground without performing any illegal or dishonest act in order to conform to the policies of the new elective officers? 4.____

   A. *No;* the opinions and beliefs of the career officials are the result of long experience in administration and are more reliable than those of politicians.
   B. *Yes;* only in this way can citizens, political officials and career administrators alike have confidence in the performance of their respective functions.
   C. *No;* a top career official who is so spineless as to change his views or procedures as a result of public opinion is of little value to the public service.
   D. *Yes;* legal or illegal, it is necessary that a city employee carry out the orders of his superior officers
   E. *No;* shifting ground with every change in administration will preclude the use of a constant overall policy

5. Participation in developing plans which will affect levels in the organization in addition to his own, will contribute to an individual's understanding of the entire system. When possible, this should be encouraged.
This policy is, in general, 5.____

   A. *desirable;* the maintenance of any organization depends upon individual understanding
   B. *undesirable;* employees should participate only in thise activities which affect their own level, otherwise conflicts in authority may arise
   C. *desirable;* an employee's will to contribute to the maintenance of an organization depends to a great extent on the level which he occupies
   D. *undesirable;* employees can be trained more efficiently and economically in an organized training program than by participating in plan development
   E. *desirable;* it will enable the employee to make intelligent suggestions for adjustment of the plan in the future

6. Constant study should be made of the information contained in reports to isolate those elements of experience which are static, those which are variable and repetitive, and those which are variable and due to chance
Knowledge of those elements of experience in his organization which are static or constant will enable the operating official to 6.____

   A. fix responsibility for their supervision at a lower level
   B. revise the procedure in order to make the elements variable
   C. arrange for follow-up and periodic adjustment
   D. bring related data together
   E. provide a frame of reference within which detailed standards for measurement can be installed

7. A chief staff officer,serving as one of the immediate advisors to the department head, has demonstrated a special capacity for achieving internal agreements and for sound judgment. As a result he has been used more and more as a source of counsel and assistance by the department head. Other staff officers and line officials as well have discovered that it is wise for them to check with this colleague in advance on all problematical matters handed up to the department head. Developments such as this are 7.____

   A. *undesirable;* they disrupt the normal lines for flow of work in an organization
   B. *desirable;* they allow an organization to make the most of its strength wherever such strength resides
   C. *undesirable;* they tend to undermine the authority of the department head and put it in the hands of a staff officer who does not have the responsibility
   D. *desirable;* they tend to resolve internal ambiguities in organization
   E. *undesirable;* they make for bad morale by causing *cutthroat* competition

8. A common difference among executives is that some are not content unless they are out in front in everything that concerns their organization, while others prefer to run things by pulling strings, by putting others out in front and by stepping into the breach only when necessary.
Generally speaking, an advantage this latter method of operation has over the former is that it 8.____

A. results in a higher level of morale over a sustained period of time
B. gets results by exhortation and direct stimulus
C. makes it unnecessary to calculate integrated moves
D. makes the personality of the executive felt further down the line
E. results in the executive getting the reputation for being a good fellow

9. Administrators frequently have to get facts by interviewing people. Although the interview is a legitimate fact gathering technique, it has definite limitations which should not be overlooked. The one of the following which is an important limitation is that 9.____

A. people who are initerviewed frequently answer questions with guesses rather than admit their ignorance
B. it is a poor way to discover the general attitude and thinking of supervisors interviewed
C. people sometimes hesitate to give information during an interview which they will submit in written form
D. it is a poor way to discover how well employees understand departmental policies
E. the material obtained from the interview can usually be obtained at lower cost from existing records

10. It is desirable and advantageous to leave a maximum measure of planning responsibility to operating agencies or units, rather than to remove the responsibility to a central planning staff agency. 10.____
Adoption of the former policy (decentralized planning) would lead to

A. *less effective planning;* operating personnel do not have the time to make long-term plans
B. *more effective planning;* operating units are usually better equipped technically than any staff agency and consequently are in a better position to set up valid plans
C. *less effective planning;* a central planning agency has a more objective point of view than any operating agency can achieve
D. *more effective planning;* plans are conceived in terms of the existing situation and their exeuction is carried out with the will to succeed
E. *less effective planning;* there is little or no opportunity to check deviation from plans in the proposed set-up

Questions 11–15.

DIRECTIONS: The following sections appeared in a report on the work production of two bureaus of a department. Base your answers to questions 11 through 15 on this information. Throughout the report, assume that each month has 4 weeks.

Each of the two bureaus maintains a chronological file. In Bureau A, every 9 months on the average, this material fills a standard legal size file cabinet sufficient for 12,000 work units. In Bureau B, the same type of cabinet is filled in 18 months. Each bureau maintains three complete years of information plus a current file. When the current file cabinet is filled, the cabinet containing the oldest material is emptied, the contents disposed of and the cabinet used for current material. The similarity of these operations makes it possible to consolidate these files with little effort.

Study of the practice of using typists as filing clerks for periods when there is no typing work showed: (1) Bureau A has for the past 6 months completed a total of 1500 filing work units a week using on the average 100 man-hours of trained file clerk time and 20 man-hours of typist time; (2) Bureau B has in the same period completed a total of 2000 filing work units a week using on the average 125 man-hours of trained file clerk time and 60 hours of typist time. This includes all work in chronological files. Assuming that all clerks work at the same speed and that all typists work at the same speed, this indicates that work other than filing should be found for typists or that they should be given some training in the filing procedures used... It should be noted that Bureau A has not been producing the 1,600 units of technical (not filing) work per 30 day period required by Schedule K,but is at present 200 units behind. The Bureau should be allowed 3 working days to get on schedule.

11. What percentage (approximate) of the total number of filing work units completed in both units consists of the work involved in the maintenance of the chronological files? 11.____

A. 5% B. 10% C. 15% D. 20% E. 25%

12. If the two chronological files are consolidated, the number of months which should be allowed for filling a cabinet is 12.____

A. 2 B. 4 C. 6 D. 8 E. 14

13. The MAXIMUM number of file cabinets which can be released for other uses as a result of the consolidation recommended is 13.____

A. 0 B. 1 C. 2 D. 3
E. not determinable on the basis of the data given

14. If all the filing work for both units is consolidated without diminution in the amount to be done and all filing work is done by trained file clerks, the number of clerks required (35-hour work week) is 14.____

A. 4 B. 5 C. 6 D. 7 E. 8

15. In order to comply with the recommendation with respect to Schedule K, the present work production of Bureau A must be increased by 15.____

A. 50% B. 100% C. 150% D. 200%
E. an amount which is not determinable

16. A certain training program during World War II resulted in the training of thousands of supervisors in industry. The methods of this program were later successfully applied in various governmental agencies. The program was based upon the assumption that there is an irreducible minimum of three supervisory skills. The ONE of these skills among the following is 16.____

A. to know how to perform the job at hand well
B. to be able to deal personally with workers, especially face to face
C. to be able to imbue workers with the will to perform the job well
D. to know the kind of work that is done by one's unit and the policies and procedures of one's agency
E. the *know-how* of administrative and supervisory processes

17. A comment made by an employee about a training course was, *We never have any idea how we are getting along in that course.* The fundamental error in training methods to which this criticism points is 17.____

A. insufficient student participation
B. failure to develop a feeling of need or active want for the material being presented
C. the training sessions may be too long
D. no attempt may have been made to connect the new material with what was already known
E. no goals have been set for the students

18. Assume that you are attending a departmental conference on efficiency ratings at which it is proposed that a man-to-man rating scale be introduced. You should point out that, of the following, the CHIEF weakness of the man-to-man rating scale is that 18.____

A. it involves abstract numbers rather than concrete employee characteristics
B. judges are unable to select their own standards for comparison
C. the standard for comparison shifts from man to man for each person rated
D. not every person rated is given the opportunity to serve as a standard for comparison
E. standards for comparison will vary from judge to judge

19. Assume that you are conferring with a supervisor who has assigned to his subordinates efficiency ratings which you believe to be generally too low. The supervisor argues that his ratings are generally low because his subordinates are generally inferior. Of the following, the evidence MOST relevant to the point at issue can be secured by comparing efficiency ratings assigned by the supervisor 19.____

A. with ratings assigned by other supervisors in the same agency
B. this year with ratings assigned by him in previous years
C. to men recently transferred to his unit with ratings previously earned by these men
D. with the general city average of ratings assigned by all supervisors to all employees
E. with the relative order of merit of his employees as determined independently by promotion test marks

20. The one of the following which is NOT among the most common of the compensable factors used in wage evaluation studies is 20.____

A. initiative and ingenuity required
B. physical demand
C. responsibility for the safety of others
D. working conditions
E. presence of avoidable hazards

21. If independent functions are separated, there is an immediate gain in conserving special skills. If we are to make optimum use of the abilities of our employees, these skills must be conserved.
Assuming the correctness of this statement, it follows that 21.____

A. if we are not making optimum use of employee abilities, independent functions have not been separated
B. we are making optimum use of employee abilities if we conserve special skills
C. we are making optimum use of employee abilities if independent functions have been separated
D. we are not making optimum use of employee abilities if we do not conserve special skills
E. if special skills are being conserved, independent functions need not be separated

22. A reorganization of the bureau to provide for a stenographic pool instead of individual unit stenographers will result in more stenographic help being available to each unit when it is required, and consequently will result in greater productivity for each unit. An analysis of the space requirements shows that setting up a stenographic pool will require a minimum of 400 square feet of good space. In order to obtain this space, it will be necessary to reduce the space available for technical personnel, resulting in lesser productivity for each unit. 22.____
On the basis of the above discussion, it can be stated that, in order to obtain greater productivity for each unit,

A. a stenographic pool should be set up
B. further analysis of the space requirement should be made
C. it is not certain as to whether or not a stenographic pool should be set up
D. the space available for each technician should be increased in order to compensate for the absence of a stenographic pool
E. a stenographic pool should not be set up

23. The adoption of a single consolidated form will mean that most of the form will not be used in any one operation. This would create waste and confusion. 23.____
This conclusion is based upon the unstated hypothesis that

A. if waste and confusion are to be avoided, a single consolidated form should be used
B. if a single consolidated form is constructed, most of it can be used in each operation
C. if waste and confusion are to be avoided, most of the form employed should be used
D. most of a single consolidated form is not used
E. a single consolidated form should not be used

KEY(CORRECT ANSWERS)

1. E
2. B
3. C
4. B
5. E
6. A
7. B
8. A
9. A
10. D
11. C
12. C
13. B
14. D
15. E
16. B
17. E
18. E
19. C
20. E
21. D
22. C
23. C

REPORT WRITING
EXAMINATION SECTION
TEST 1

DIRECTIONS: Each question or incomplete statement is followed by several suggested answers or completions. Select the one that BEST answers the question or completes the statement. *PRINT THE LETTER OF THE CORRECT ANSWER IN THE SPACE AT THE RIGHT.*

Questions 1-4.

DIRECTIONS: Answer Questions 1 through 4 on the basis of the following report which was prepared by a supervisor for inclusion in his agency's annual report.

On Oct. 13, I was assigned to study the salaries paid to clerical employees in various titles by the city and by private industry in the area.

In order to get the data I needed, I called Mr. Johnson at the Bureau of the Budget and the payroll officers at X Corp.—a brokerage house, Y Co.—an insurance company, and Z Inc.—a publishing firm. None of them was available and I had to call all of them again the next day.

When I finally got the information I needed, I drew up a chart, which is attached. Note that not all of the companies I contacted employed people at all the different levels used in the city service.

The conclusions I draw from analyzing this information is as follows: The city's entry-level salary is about average for the region; middle-level salaries are generally higher in the city government than in private industry; but salaries at the highest levels in private industry are better than city employees' pay.

1. Which of the following criticisms about the style in which this report is written is *most valid*? 1.____

   A. It is too informal.
   B. It is too concise.
   C. It is too choppy.
   D. The syntax is too complex.

2. Judging from the statements made in the report, the method followed by this employee in performing his research was 2.____

   A. *good;* he contacted a representative sample of businesses in the area
   B. *poor;* he should have drawn more definite conclusions
   C. *good;* he was persistent in collecting information
   D. *poor;* he did not make a thorough study

3. One sentence in this report contains a grammatical error. This sentence *begins* on line number 3.___

   A. 4 B. 7 C. 10 D. 13

4. The type of information given in this report which should be presented in footnotes or in an appendix, is the 4.___

   A. purpose of the study
   B. specifics about the businesses contacted
   C. reference to the chart
   D. conclusions drawn by the author

5. The use of a graph to show statistical data in a report is *superior* to a table because it 5.___

   A. features approximations
   B. emphasizes facts and relationships more dramatically
   C. C. presents data more accurately
   D. is easily understood by the average reader

6. Of the following, the degree of formality required of a written report in tone is *most likely* to depend on the 6.___

   A. subject matter of the report
   B. frequency of its occurrence
   C. amount of time available for its preparation
   D. audience for whom the report is intended

7. Of the following, a distinguishing characteristic of a written report intended for the head of your agency as compared to a report prepared for a lower-echelon staff member, is that the report for the agency head should *usually* include 7.___

   A. considerably more detail, especially statistical data
   B. the essential details in an abbreviated form
   C. all available source material
   D. an annotated bibliography

8. Assume that you are asked to write a lengthy report for use by the administrator of your agency, the subject of which is "The Impact of Proposed New Data Processing Operations on Line Personnel" in your agency. You decide that the *most appropriate* type of report for you to prepare is an analytical report, including recommendations.
   The MAIN reason for your decision is that 8.___

   A. the subject of the report is extremely complex
   B. large sums of money are involved
   C. the report is being prepared for the administrator
   D. you intend to include charts and graphs

9. Assume that you are preparing a report based on a survey dealing with the attitudes of employees in Division X regarding proposed new changes in compensating employees for working overtime. Three per cent of the respondents to the survey voluntarily offer an unfavorable opinion on the method of assigning overtime work, a question not specifically asked of the employees. 9.____
On the basis of this information, the *most appropriate* and *significant* of the following comments for you to make in the report with regard to employees' attitudes on assigning overtime work, is that

   A. an insignificant percentage of employees dislike the method of assigning overtime work
   B. three per cent of the employees in Division X dislike the method of assigning overtime work
   C. three per cent of the sample selected for the survey voiced an unfavorable opinion on the method of assigning overtime work
   D. some employees voluntarily voiced negative feelings about the method of assigning overtime work, making it impossible to determine the extent of this attitude

10. A supervisor should be able to prepare a report that is well-written and unambiguous. Of the following sentences that might appear in a report, select the one which communicates *most clearly* the intent of its author. 10.____

   A. When your subordinates speak to a group of people, they should be well-informed.
   B. When he asked him to leave, SanMan King told him that he would refuse the request.
   C. Because he is a good worker, Foreman Jefferson assigned Assistant Foreman D'Agostino to replace him.
   D. Each of us is responsible for the actions of our subordinates.

11. In some reports, especially longer ones, a list of the resources (books, papers, magazines, etc.) used to prepare it is included. This list is called the 11.____

   A. accreditation
   B. bibliography
   C. summary
   D. glossary

12. Reports are usually divided into several sections, some of which are more necessary than others. 12.____
Of the following, the section which is ABSOLUTELY necessary to include in a report is

   A. a table of contents
   B. the body
   C. an index
   D. a bibliography

13. Suppose you are writing a report on an interview you have just completed with a particularly hostile applicant. Which of the following BEST describes what you should include in this report? 13.____

   A. What you think caused the applicant's hostile attitude during the interview
   B. Specific examples of the applicant's hostile remarks and behavior
   C. The relevant information uncovered during the interview
   D. A recommendation that the applicant's request be denied because of his hostility

14. When including recommendations in a report to your supervisor, which of the following is MOST important for you to do? 14.____

    A. Provide several alternative courses of action for each recommendation
    B. First present the supporting evidence, then the recommendations
    C. First present the recommendations, then the supporting evidence
    D. Make sure the recommendations arise logically out of the information in the report

15. It is often necessary that the writer of a report present facts and sufficient arguments to gain acceptance of the points, conclusions, or recommendations set forth in the report. Of the following, the LEAST advisable step to take in organizing a report, when such argumentation is the important factor, is a(n) 15.____

    A. elaborate expression of personal belief
    B. businesslike discussion of the problem as a whole
    C. orderly arrangement of convincing data
    D. reasonable explanation of the primary issues

16. In some types of reports, visual aids add interest, meaning, and support. They also provide an essential means of effectively communicating the message of the report. Of the following, the selection of the suitable visual aids to use with a report is LEAST dependent on the 16.____

    A. nature and scope of the report
    B. way in which the aid is to be used
    C. aids used in other reports
    D. prospective readers of the report

17. Visual aids used in a report may be placed either in the text material or in the appendix. Deciding where to put a chart, table, or any such aid *should* depend on the 17.____

    A. title of the report
    B. purpose of the visual aid
    C. title of the visual aid
    D. length of the report

18. A report is often revised several times before final preparation and distribution in an effort to make certain the report meets the needs of the situation for which it is designed. Which of the following is the BEST way for the author to be sure that a report covers the areas he intended? 18.____

    A. Obtain a co-worker's opinion
    B. Compare it with a content checklist
    C. Test it on a subordinate
    D. Check his bibliography

19. In which of the following situations is an oral report preferable to a written report? When a(n) 19.____

    A. recommendation is being made for a future plan of action
    B. department head requests immediate information
    C. long standing policy change is made
    D. analysis of complicated statistical data is involved

20. When an applicant is approved, the supervisor must fill in standard forms with certain information. 20.____
The GREATEST advantage of using standard forms in this situation rather than having the supervisor write the report as he sees fit, is that

A. the report can be acted on quickly
B. the report can be written without directions from a supervisor
C. needed information is less likely to be left out of the report
D. information that is written up this way is more likely to be verified

21. Assume that it is part of your job to prepare a monthly report for your unit head that eventually goes to the director. The report contains information on the number of applicants you have interviewed that have been approved and the number of applicants you have interviewed that have been turned down. 21.____
Errors on such reports are serious because

A. you are expected to be able to prove how many applicants you have interviewed each month
B. accurate statistics are needed for effective management of the department
C. they may not be discovered before the report is transmitted to the director
D. they may result in loss to the applicants left out of the report

22. The frequency with which job reports are submitted should depend MAINLY on 22.____

A. how comprehensive the report has to be
B. the amount of information in the report
C. the availability of an experienced man to write the report
D. the importance of changes in the information included in the report

23. The CHIEF purpose in preparing an outline for a report is *usually* to insure that 23.____

A. the report will be grammatically correct
B. every point will be given equal emphasis
C. principal and secondary points will be properly integrated
D. the language of the report will be of the same level and include the same technical terms

24. The MAIN reason for requiring written job reports is to 24.____

A. avoid the necessity of oral orders
B. develop better methods of doing the work
C. provide a permanent record of what was done
D. increase the amount of work that can be done

25. Assume you are recommending in a report to your supervisor that a radical change in a standard maintenance procedure should be adopted. 25.____
Of the following, the MOST important information to be included in this report is

A. a list of the reasons for making this change
B. the names of others who favor the change
C. a complete description of the present procedure
D. amount of training time needed for the new procedure

KEY (CORRECT ANSWERS)

1. A
2. D
3. D
4. B
5. B

6. D
7. B
8. A
9. D
10. D

11. B
12. B
13. C
14. D
15. A

16. C
17. B
18. B
19. B
20. C

21. B
22. D
23. C
24. C
25. A

TEST 2

DIRECTIONS: Each question or incomplete statement is followed by several suggested answers or completions. Select the one that BEST answers the question or completes the statement. *PRINT THE LETTER OF THE CORRECT ANSWER IN THE SPACE AT THE RIGHT.*

1. It is often necessary that the writer of a report present facts and sufficient arguments to gain acceptance of the points, conclusions, or recommendations set forth in the report. Of the following, the LEAST advisable step to take in organizing a report, when such argumentation is the important factor, is a(n) 1.____

   A. elaborate expression of personal belief
   B. businesslike discussion of the problem as a whole
   C. orderly arrangement of convincing data
   D. reasonable explanation of the primary issues

2. Of the following, the factor which is generally considered to be LEAST characteristic of a good control report is that it 2.____

   A. stresses performance that adheres to standard rather than emphasizing the exception
   B. supplies information intended to serve as the basis for corrective action
   C. provides feedback for the planning process
   D. includes data that reflect trends as well as current status

3. An administrative assistant has been asked by his superior to write a concise, factual report with objective conclusions and recommendations based on facts assembled by other researchers. 3.____
   Of the following factors, the administrative assistant should give LEAST consideratio to

   A. the educational level of the person or persons for whom the report is being prepared
   B. the use to be made of the report
   C. the complexity of the problem
   D. his own feelings about the importance of the problem

4. When making a written report, it is often recommended that the findings or conclusions be presented near the beginning of the report. 4.____
   Of the following, the MOST important reason for doing this is that it

   A. facilitates organizing the material clearly
   B. assures that all the topics will be covered
   C. avoids unnecessary repetition of ideas
   D. prepares the reader for the facts that will follow

5. You have been asked to write a report on methods of hiring and training new employees. Your report is going to be about ten pages long. 5.____
   For the convenience of your readers, a brief summary of your findings *should*

   A. appear at the beginning of your report
   B. be appended to the report as a postscript
   C. be circulated in a separate memo
   D. be inserted in tabular form in the middle of your report

6. In preparing a report, the MAIN reason for writing an outline is *usually* to 6.___

   A. help organize thoughts in a logical sequence
   B. provide a guide for the typing of the report
   C. allow the ultimate user to review the report in advance
   D. ensure that the report is being prepared on schedule

7. The one of the following which is *most appropriate* as a reason for including footnotes in a report is to 7.___

   A. correct capitalization
   B. delete passages
   C. improve punctuation
   D. cite references

8. A completed formal report may contain all of the following EXCEPT 8.___

   A. a synopsis
   B. a preface
   C. marginal notes
   D. bibliographical references

9. Of the following, the MAIN use of proofreaders' marks is to 9.___

   A. explain corrections to be made
   B. indicate that a manuscript has been read and approved
   C. let the reader know who proofread the report
   D. indicate the format of the report

10. Informative, readable and concise reports have been found to observe the following rules: 10.___

    Rule I. Keep the report short and easy to understand.
    Rule II. Vary the length of sentences.
    Rule III. Vary the style of sentences so that, for example, they are not all just sub ject-verb, subject-verb.

    Consider this hospital laboratory report: The experiment was started in January. The apparatus was put together in six weeks. At that time the synthesizing process was begun. The synthetic chemicals were separated. Then they were used in tests on patients.

    Which one of the following choices MOST accurately classifies the above rules into those which are *violated* by this report and those which are *not*?

    A. II is violated, but I and III are not.
    B. III is violated, but I and II are not.
    C. II and III are violated, but I is not.
    D. I, II, and III are violated.

Questions 11-13.

DIRECTIONS: Questions 11 through 13 are based on the following example of a report. The report consists of eight numbered sentences, some of which are not consistent with the principles of good report writing.

(1) I interviewed Mrs. Loretta Crawford in Room 424 of County Hospital. (2) She had collapsed on the street and been brought into emergency. (3) She is an attractive woman with many friends judging by the cards she had received. (4) She did not know what her husband's last job had been, or what their present income was. (5) The first thing that Mrs. Crawford said was that she had never worked and that her husband was presently unemployed. (6) She did not know if they had any medical coverage or if they could pay the bill. (7) She said that her husband could not be reached by telephone but that he would be in to see her that afternoon. (8) I left word at the nursing station to be called when he arrived.

11. A good report should be arranged in logical order. Which of the following sentences from the report does NOT appear in its proper sequence in the report? Sentence 11.____

A. 1 B. 4 C. 7 D. 8

12. Only material that is relevant to the main thought of a report should be included. Which of the following sentences from the report contains material which is LEAST relevant to this report? Sentence 12.____

A. 3 B. 4 C. 6 D. 8

13. Reports should include all essential information. Of the following, the MOST important fact that is *missing* from this report is: 13.____

A. Who was involved in the interview
B. What was discovered at the interview
C. When the interview took place
D. Where the interview took place

Questions 14-15.

DIRECTIONS: Each of Questions 14 and 15 consists of four numbered sentences which constitute a paragraph in a report. They are not in the right order. Choose the numbered arrangement appearing after letter A, B, C, or D which is MOST logical and which BEST expresses the thought of the paragraph.

14. 14.____

I. Congress made the commitment explicit in the Housing Act of 1949, establishing as a national goal the realization of a decent home and suitable environment for every American family.
II. The result has been that the goal of decent home and suitable environment is still as far distant as ever for the disadvantaged urban family.
III. In spite of this action by Congress, federal housing programs have continued to be fragmented and grossly under-funded.
IV. The passage of the National Housing Act signaled a new federal commitment to provide housing for the nation's citizens.

A. I, IV, III, II
B. IV, I, III, II
C. IV, I, III, II
D. II, IV, I, III

15. I. The greater expense does not necessarily involve "exploitation," but it is often perceived as exploitative and unfair by those who are aware of the price differences involved, but unaware of operating costs. 15.___

II. Ghetto residents believe they are "exploited" by local merchants, and evidence substantiates some of these beliefs.

III. However, stores in low-income areas were more likely to be small independents, which could not achieve the economies available to supermarket chains and were, therefore, more likely to charge higher prices, and the customers were more likely to buy smaller-sized packages which are more expensive per unit of measure.

IV. A study conducted in one city showed that distinctly higher prices were charged for goods sold in ghetto stores than in other areas.

A. IV, II, I, III
B. IV, I, III, II
C. II, IV, III, I
D. II, III, IV, I

16. In organizing data to be presented in a formal report, the FIRST of the following steps should be 16.___

A. determining the conclusions to be drawn
B. establishing the time sequence of the data
C. sorting and arranging like data into groups
D. evaluating how consistently the data support the recommendations

17. All reports should be prepared with *at least* one copy so that 17.___

A. there is one copy for your file
B. there is a copy for your supervisor
C. the report can be sent to more than one person
D. the person getting the report can forward a copy to someone else

18. Before turning in a report of an investigation he has made, a supervisor discovers some additional information he did not include in this report. 18.___
Whether he rewrites this report to include this additional information should PRIMARILY depend on the

A. importance of the report itself
B. number of people who will eventually review this report
C. established policy covering the subject matter of the report
D. bearing this new information has on the conclusions of the report

---

KEY (CORRECT ANSWERS)

1. A
2. A
3. D
4. D
5. A

6. A
7. D
8. C
9. A
10. C

11. B
12. A
13. C
14. B
15. C

16. C
17. A
18. D

PRINCIPLES AND PRACTICES OF ADMINISTRATION, SUPERVISION & MANAGEMENT

TABLE OF CONTENTS

	Page
GENERAL ADMINISTRATION	1
SEVEN BASIC FUNCTIONS OF THE SUPERVISOR	2
1. Planning	2
2. Organizing	3
3. Staffing	3
4. Directing	3
5. Coordinating	3
6. Reporting	3
7. Budgeting	3
PLANNING TO MEET MANAGEMENT GOALS	4
I. What is Planning?	4
II. Who Should Make Plans?	4
III. What are the Results of Poor Planning?	4
IV. Principles of Planning	4
MANAGEMENT PRINCIPLES	5
I. Management	5
II. Management Principles	5
III. Organization Structure	6
ORGANIZATION	8
PRINCIPLES OF ORGANIZATION	9
1. Definition	9
2. Purpose of Organization	9
3. Basic Considerations in Organizational Planning	9
4. Bases for Organization	10
5. Assignment of Functions	10
6. Delegation of Authority and Responsibility	10
7. Employee Relationships	10
DELEGATING	11
REPORTS	11

MANAGEMENT CONTROLS 12
1. Control 12
2. Basis for Control 13
3. Policy 13
4. Procedure 13
5. Basis of Control 14

FRAMEWORK OF MANAGEMENT 14

PROBLEM SOLVING 16
1. Identify the Problem 16
2. Gather Data 17
3. List Possible Solutions 17
4. Test Possible Solutions 17
5. Select the Best Solution 18
6. Put the Solution Into Actual Practice 18

COMMUNICATION 19
1. What is Communication? 19
2. Why is Communication Needed? 19
3. How is Communication Achieved? 19
4. Why Does Communication Fail? 20
5. How to Improve Communication? 20
6. How to Determine if You Are Getting Across 21
7. The Key Attitude 21

FUNCTIONS OF A DEPARTMENT PERSONNEL OFFICE 22

SUPERVISION 23
1. The Authoritarian Approach 23
2. The Laissez-Faire Approach 23
3. The Democratic Approach 24

EMPLOYEE MORALE 25

MOTIVATION 25

EMPLOYEE PARTICIPATION 26

STEPS IN HANDLING A GRIEVANCE 27

DISCIPLINE 28

PRINCIPLES AND PRACTICES OF ADMINISTRATION, SUPERVISION & MANAGEMENT

Most people are inclined to think of administration as something that only a few persons are responsible for in a large organization. Perhaps this is true if you are thinking of Administration with a capital *A*, but administration with a lower case a is a responsibility of supervisors at all levels each working day.

All of us feel we are pretty good supervisors and that we do a good job of administering the workings of our agency. By and large, this is true, but every so often it is good to check up on ourselves. Checklists appear from time to time in various publications which psychologists say, tell whether or not a person will make a good wife, husband, doctor, lawyer, or supervisor.

The following questions are an excellent checklist to test yourself as a supervisor and administrator.

Remember, Administration gives direction and points the way but administration carries the ideas to fruition. Each is dependent on the other for its success. Remember, too, that no unit is too small for these departmental functions to be carried out. These statements apply equally as well to the Chief Librarian as to the Department Head with but one or two persons to supervise.

<u>GENERAL ADMINISTRATION</u> - General Responsibilities of Supervisors

1. Have I prepared written statements of functions, activities, and duties for my organizational unit?

2. Have I prepared procedural guides for operating activities?

3. Have I established clearly in writing, lines of authority and responsibility for my organizational unit?

4. Do I make recommendations for improvements in organization, policies, administrative and operating routines and procedures, including simplification of work and elimination of non-essential operations?

5. Have I designated and trained an understudy to function in my absence?

6. Do I supervise and train personnel within the unit to effectively perform their assignments?

7. Do I assign personnel and distribute work on such a basis as to carry out the organizational unit's assignment or mission in the most effective and efficient manner?

8. Have I established administrative controls by:

    a. Fixing responsibility and accountability on all supervisors under my direction for the proper performance of their functions and duties.

b. Preparing and submitting periodic work load and progress reports covering the operations of the unit to my immediate superior.

c. Analysis and evaluation of such reports received from subordinate units.

d. Submission of significant developments and problems arising within the organizational unit to my immediate superior.

e. Conducting conferences, inspections, etc., as to the status and efficiency of unit operations.

9. Do I maintain an adequate and competent working force?

10. Have I fostered good employee-department relations, seeing that established rules, regulations, and instructions are being carried out properly?

11. Do I collaborate and consult with other organizational units performing related functions to insure harmonious and efficient working relationships?

12. Do I maintain liaison through prescribed channels with city departments and other governmental agencies concerned with the activities of the unit?

13. Do I maintain contact with and keep abreast of the latest developments and techniques of administration (professional societies, groups, periodicals, etc.) as to their applicability to the activities of the unit?

14. Do I communicate with superiors and subordinates through prescribed organizational channels?

15. Do I notify superiors and subordinates in instances where bypassing is necessary as soon thereafter as practicable?

16. Do I keep my superior informed of significant developments and problems?

SEVEN BASIC FUNCTIONS OF THE SUPERVISOR

1. PLANNING
This means working out goals and means to obtain goals. What needs to be done, who will do it, how, when, and where it is to be done.

SEVEN STEPS IN PLANNING

1. Define job or problem clearly.
2. Consider priority of job.
3. Consider time-limit - starting and completing.
4. Consider minimum distraction to, or interference with, other activities.
5. Consider and provide for contingencies - possible emergencies.
6. Break job down into components.
7. Consider the 5 W's and H:

WHY ... is it necessary to do the job? (Is the purpose clearly defined?)
WHAT ... needs to be done to accomplish the defined purpose?
... is needed to do the job? (money, materials, etc.)
WHO ... is needed to do the job?
... will have responsibilities?
WHERE ... is the work to be done?
WHEN ... is the job to begin and end? (schedules, etc.)
HOW ... is the job to be done? (methods, controls, records, etc.)

2. ORGANIZING
This means dividing up the work, establishing clear lines of responsibility and authority and coordinating efforts to get the job done.

3. STAFFING
The whole personnel function of bringing in and training staff, getting the right man and fitting him to the right job - the job to which he is best suited.
In the normal situation, the supervisor's responsibility regarding staffing normally includes providing accurate job descriptions, that is, duties of the jobs, requirements, education and experience, skills, physical, etc.; assigning the work for maximum use of skills; and proper utilization of the probationary period to weed out unsatisfactory employees.

4. DIRECTING
Providing the necessary leadership to the group supervised. Important work gets done to the supervisor's satisfaction.

5. COORDINATING
The all-important duty of inter-relating the various parts of the work.
The supervisor is also responsible for controlling the coordinated activities. This means measuring performance according to a time schedule and setting quotas to see that the goals previously set are being reached. Reports from workers should be analyzed, evaluated, and made part of all future plans.

6. REPORTING
This means proper and effective communication to your superiors, subordinates, and your peers (in definition of the job of the supervisor). Reports should be read and information contained therein should be used not be filed away and forgotten. Reports should be written in such a way that the desired action recommended by the report is forthcoming.

7. BUDGETING
This means controlling current costs and forecasting future costs. This forecast is based on past experience, future plans and programs, as well as current costs.

You will note that these seven functions can fall under three topics:

Planning)
Organizing) Make a Plan

Staffing)
Directing) Get things done
Controlling)

Reporting)
Budgeting) Watch it work

PLANNING TO MEET MANAGEMENT GOALS

I. WHAT IS PLANNING?
   A. Thinking a job through before new work is done to determine the best way to do it
   B. A method of doing something
   C. Ways and means for achieving set goals
   D. A means of enabling a supervisor to deliver with a minimum of effort, all details involved in coordinating his work

II. WHO SHOULD MAKE PLANS?
Everybody!
All levels of supervision must plan work. (Top management, heads of divisions or bureaus, first line supervisors, and individual employees.) The higher the level, the more planning required.

III. WHAT ARE THE RESULTS OF POOR PLANNING?
   A. Failure to meet deadline
   B. Low employee morale
   C. Lack of job coordination
   D. Overtime is frequently necessary
   E. Excessive cost, waste of material and manhours

IV. PRINCIPLES OF PLANNING
   A. Getting a clear picture of your objectives. What exactly are you trying to accomplish?
   B. Plan the whole job, then the parts, in proper sequence.
   C. Delegate the planning of details to those responsible for executing them.
   D. Make your plan flexible.
   E. Coordinate your plan with the plans of others so that the work may be processed with a minimum of delay.
   F. Sell your plan before you execute it.
   G. Sell your plan to your superior, subordinate, in order to gain maximum participation and coordination.
   H. Your plan should take precedence. Use knowledge and skills that others have brought to a similar job.
   I. Your plan should take account of future contingencies; allow for future expansion.
   J. Plans should include minor details. Leave nothing to chance that can be anticipated.
   K. Your plan should be simple and provide standards and controls. Establish quality and quantity standards and set a standard method of doing the job. The controls will indicate whether the job is proceeding according to plan.
   L. Consider possible bottlenecks, breakdowns, or other difficulties that are likely to arise.

V. Q. WHAT ARE THE *YARDSTICKS* BY WHICH PLANNING SHOULD BE MEASURED?
   A. Any plan should:
      - Clearly state a definite course of action to be followed and goal to be achieved, with consideration for emergencies.
      - Be realistic and practical.

- State what's to be done, when it's to be done, where, how, and by whom.
- Establish the most efficient sequence of operating steps so that more is accomplished in less time, with the least effort, and with the best quality results.
- Assure meeting deliveries without delays.
- Establish the standard by which performance is to be judged.

Q. WHAT KINDS OF PLANS DOES EFFECTIVE SUPERVISION REQUIRE?
A. Plans should cover such factors as:
- Manpower - right number of properly trained employees on the job.
- Materials - adequate supply of the right materials and supplies.
- Machines - full utilization of machines and equipment, with proper maintenance.
- Methods - most efficient handling of operations.
- Deliveries - making deliveries on time.
- Tools - sufficient well-conditioned tools
- Layout - most effective use of space.
- Reports - maintaining proper records and reports.
- Supervision - planning work for employees and organizing supervisor's own time.

I. MANAGEMENT

Question: *What do we mean by management?*

Answer: *Getting work done through others.*

Management could also be defined as planning, directing, and controlling the operations of a bureau or division so that all factors will function properly and all persons cooperate efficiently for a common objective.

II. MANAGEMENT PRINCIPLES

1. There should be a hierarchy - wherein authority and responsibility run upward and downward through several levels - with a broad base at the bottom and a single head at the top.

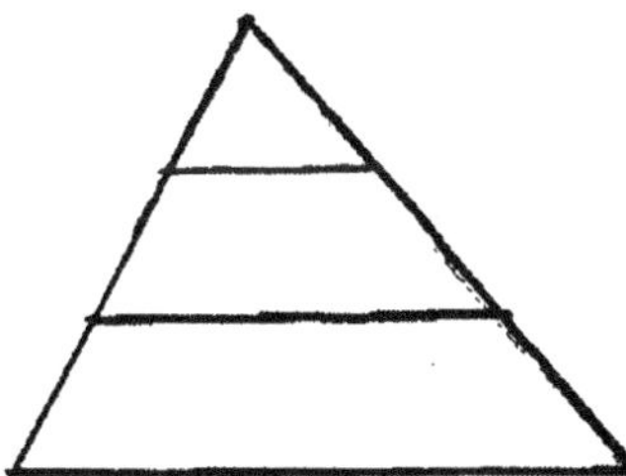

2. Each and every unit or person in the organization should be answerable ultimately to the manager at the apex. In other words, *The buck stops here!*

3. Every necessary function involved in the bureau's objectives is assigned to a unit in that bureau.
4. Responsibilities assigned to a unit are specifically clear-cut and understood.

5. Consistent methods of organizational structure should be applied at each level of the organization.

6. Each member of the bureau from top to bottom knows:
   to whom he reports
   who reports to him.

7. No member of one bureau reports to more than one supervisor.
   No dual functions

8. Responsibility for a function is matched by authority necessary to perform that function.
   Weight of authority

9. Individuals or units reporting to a supervisor do not exceed the number which can be feasibly and effectively coordinated and directed.
   Concept of *span of control*

10. Channels of command (management) are not violated by staff units, although there should be staff services to facilitate and coordinate management functions.

11. Authority and responsibility should be decentralized to units and individuals who are responsible for the actual performance of operations.
    Welfare - down to Welfare Centers
    Hospitals - down to local hospitals

12. Management should exercise control through attention to policy problems of exceptional importance, rather than through review of routine actions of subordinates.

13. Organizations should never be permitted to grow so elaborate as to hinder work accomplishments.
    Empire building

II. ORGANIZATION STRUCTURE

Types of Organizations.

The purest form is a leader and a few followers, such as:

Supervisor

Worker | Worker | Worker | Worker

(Refer to organization chart) from supervisor to workers.

The line of authority is direct, The workers know exactly where they stand in relation to their boss, to whom they report for instructions and direction.

Unfortunately, in our present complex society, few organizations are similar to this example of a pure line organization. In this era of specialization, other people are often needed in the simplest of organizations. These specialists are known as staff. The sole purpose for their existence (staff) is to assist, advise, suggest, help or counsel line organizations. Staff has no authority to direct line people - nor do they give them direct instructions.

SUPERVISOR

Personnel	Accounting	Inspection	Legal
Worker	Worker	Worker	Worker

Line Functions		Staff Functions	
1.	Directs	1.	Advises
2.	Orders	2.	Persuades and sells
3.	Responsibility for carrying out activities from beginning to end	3.	Staff studies, reports, recommends but does not carry out
4.	Follows chain of command	4.	May advise across department lines
5.	Is identified with what it does	5.	May find its ideas identified with others
6.	Decides when and how to use staff advice	6.	Has to persuade line to want its advice
7.	Line executes	7.	Staff - Conducts studies and research. Provides advice and instructions in technical matters. Serves as technical specialist to render specific services

Types and Functions of Organization Charts.
An organization chart is a picture of the arrangement and inter-relationship of the subdivisions of an organization.

1. Types of Charts:
   a. Structural - basic relationships only
   b. Functional - includes functions or duties
   c. Personnel - positions, salaries, status, etc.
   d. Process Chart - work performed
   e. Gantt Chart - actual performance against planned
   f. Flow Chart - flow and distribution of work

2. Functions of Charts:
   a. Assist in management planning and control
   b. Indicate duplication of functions
   c. Indicate incorrect stressing of functions
   d. Indicate neglect of important functions
   e. Correct unclear authority
   f. Establish proper span of control

3. Limitations of Charts:
   a. Seldom maintained on current basis

b. Chart is oversimplified
c. Human factors cannot adequately be charted

4. Organization Charts should be:
   a. Simple
   b. Symmetrical
   c. Indicate authority
   d. Line and staff relationship differentiated
   e. Chart should be dated and bear signature of approving officer
   f. Chart should be displayed, not hidden

ORGANIZATION

There are four basic principles of organization:

1. Unity of command
2. Span of control
3. Uniformity of assignment
4. Assignment of responsibility and delegation of authority

<u>Unity of Command</u>

Unity of command means that each person in the organization should receive orders from one, and only one, supervisor. When a person has to take orders from two or more people, (a) the orders may be in conflict and the employee is upset because he does not know which he should obey, or, (b) different orders may reach him at the same time and he does not know which he should carry out first.

Equally as bad as having two bosses is the situation where the supervisor is by-passed. Let us suppose you are a supervisor whose boss by-passes you (deals directly with people reporting to you). To the worker, it is the same as having two bosses; but to you, the supervisor, it is equally serious. By-passing on the part of your boss will undermine your authority, and the people under you will begin looking to your boss for decisions and even for routine orders.

You can prevent by-passing by telling the people you supervise that if anyone tries to give them orders, they should direct that person to you.

<u>Span of Control</u>

Span of control on a given level involves:

a. The number of people being supervised
b. The distance
c. The time involved in supervising the people. (One supervisor cannot supervise too many workers effectively.)

Span of control means that a supervisor has the right number (not too many and not too few) of subordinates that he can supervise well.

<u>Uniformity of Assignment</u>

In assigning work, you as the supervisor should assign to each person jobs that are similar in nature. An employee who is assigned too many different types of jobs will waste time in going from one kind of work to another. It takes time for him to get to top production in one kind of task and, before he does so, he has to start on another.

When you assign work to people, remember that:

a. Job duties should be definite. Make it clear from the beginning what they are to do, how they are to do it, and why they are to do it. Let them know how much they are expected to do and how well they are expected to do it.

b. Check your assignments to be certain that there are no workers with too many unrelated duties, and that no two people have been given overlapping responsibilities. Your aim should be to have every task assigned to a specific person with the work fairly distributed and with each person doing his part.

Assignment of Responsibility and Delegation of Authority

A supervisor cannot delegate his final responsibility for the work of his department. The experienced supervisor knows that he gets his work done through people. He can't do it all himself. So he must assign the work and the responsibility for the work to his employees. Then they must be given the authority to carry out their responsibilities.

By assigning responsibility and delegating authority to carry out the responsibility, the supervisor builds in his workers initiative, resourcefulness, enthusiasm, and interest in their work. He is treating them as responsible adults. They can find satisfaction in their work, and they will respect the supervisor and be loyal to the supervisor.

PRINCIPLES OF ORGANIZATION

1. Definition
   Organization is the method of dividing up the work to provide the best channels for coordinated effort to get the agency's mission accomplished.

2. Purpose of Organization
   a. To enable each employee within the organization to clearly know his responsibilities and relationships to his fellow employees and to organizational units.
   b. To avoid conflicts of authority and overlapping of jurisdiction.
   c. To ensure teamwork.

3. Basic Considerations in Organizational Planning
   a. The basic plans and objectives of the agency should be determined, and the organizational structure should be adapted to carry out effectively such plans and objectives.
   b. The organization should be built around the major functions of the agency and not individuals or groups of individuals.
   c. The organization should be sufficiently flexible to meet new and changing conditions which may be brought about from within or outside the department.
   d. The organizational structure should be as simple as possible and the number of organizational units kept at a minimum.
   e. The number of levels of authority should be kept at a minimum. Each additional management level lengthens the chain of authority and responsibility and increases the time for instructions to be distributed to operating levels and for decisions to be obtained from higher authority.

f. The form of organization should permit each executive to exercise maximum initiative within the limits of delegated authority.

4. Bases for Organization
   a. Purpose (Examples: education, police, sanitation)
   b. Process (Examples: accounting, legal, purchasing)
   c. Clientele (Examples: welfare, parks, veteran)
   d. Geographic (Examples: borough offices, precincts, libraries)

5. Assignments of Functions
   a. Every function of the agency should be assigned to a specific organizational unit. Under normal circumstances, no single function should be assigned to more than one organizational unit.
   b. There should be no overlapping, duplication, or conflict between organizational elements.
   c. Line functions should be separated from staff functions, and proper emphasis should be placed on staff activities.
   d. Functions which are closely related or similar should normally be assigned to a single organizational unit.
   e. Functions should be properly distributed to promote balance, and to avoid overemphasis of less important functions and underemphasis of more essential functions.

6. Delegation of Authority and Responsibility
   a. Responsibilities assigned to a specific individual or organizational unit should carry corresponding authority, and all statements of authority or limitations thereof should be as specific as possible.
   b. Authority and responsibility for action should be decentralized to organizational units and individuals responsible for actual performance to the greatest extent possible, without relaxing necessary control over policy or the standardization of procedures. Delegation of authority will be consistent with decentralization of responsibility but such delegation will not divest an executive in higher authority of his overall responsibility.
   c. The heads of organizational units should concern themselves with important matters and should delegate to the maximum extent details and routines performed in the ordinary course of business.
   d. All responsibilities, authorities, and relationships should be stated in simple language to avoid misinterpretation.
   e. Each individual or organizational unit charged with a specific responsibility will be held responsible for results.

7. Employee Relationships
   a. The employees reporting to one executive should not exceed the number which can be effectively directed and coordinated. The number will depend largely upon the scope and extent of the responsibilities of the subordinates.
   b. No person should report to more than one supervisor. Every supervisor should know who reports to him, and every employee should know to whom he reports. Channels of authority and responsibility should not be violated by staff units.
   c. Relationships between organizational units within the agency and with outside organizations and associations should be clearly stated and thoroughly understood to avoid misunderstanding.

11

DELEGATING

1. What is Delegating?
   Delegating is assigning a job to an employee, giving him the authority to get that job done, and giving him the responsibility for seeing to it that the job is done.

   a. What to Delegate
      (1) Routine details
      (2) Jobs which may be necessary and take a lot of time, but do not have to be done by the supervisor personally (preparing reports, attending meetings, etc.)
      (3) Routine decision-making (making decisions which do not require the supervisor's personal attention)

   b. What Not to Delegate
      (1) Job details which are *executive functions* (setting goals, organizing employees into a good team, analyzing results so as to plan for the future)
      (2) Disciplinary power (handling grievances, preparing service ratings, reprimands, etc.)
      (3) Decision-making which involves large numbers of employees or other bureaus and departments
      (4) Final and complete responsibility for the job done by the unit being supervised

   c. Why Delegate?
      (1) To strengthen the organization by developing a greater number of skilled employees
      (2) To improve the employee's performance by giving him the chance to learn more about the job, handle some responsibility, and become more interested in getting the job done
      (3) To improve a supervisor's performance by relieving him of routine jobs and giving him more time for *executive functions* (planning, organizing, controlling, etc.) which cannot be delegated

2. To Whom to Delegate
   People with abilities not being used. Selection should be based on ability, not on favoritism.

REPORTS

Definition

A report is an orderly presentation of factual information directed to a specific reader for a specific purpose.

Purpose

The general purpose of a report is to bring to the reader useful and factual information about a condition or a problem. Some specific purposes of a report may be:

1. To enable the reader to appraise the efficiency or effectiveness of a person or an operation
2. To provide a basis for establishing standards
3. To reflect the results of expenditures of time, effort, and money
4. To provide a basis for developing or altering programs

Types
1. Information Report - Contains facts arranged in sequence
2. Summary (Examination) Report - Contains facts plus an analysis or discussion of the significance of the facts. Analysis may give advantages and disadvantages or give qualitative and quantitative comparisons
3. Recommendation Report - Contains facts, analysis, and conclusion logically drawn from the facts and analysis, plus a recommendation based upon the facts, analysis, and conclusions

Factors to Consider Before Writing Report

1. Why write the report - The purpose of the report should be clearly defined.
2. Who will read the report - What level of language should be used? Will the reader understand professional or technical language?
3. What should be said - What does the reader need or want to know about the subject?
4. How should it be said - Should the subject be presented tactfully? Convincingly? In a stimulating manner?

Preparatory Steps

1. Assemble the facts - Find out who, why, what, where, when, and how.
2. Organize the facts - Eliminate unnecessary information.
3. Prepare an outline - Check for orderliness, logical sequence.
4. Prepare a draft - Check for correctness, clearness, completeness, conciseness, and tone.
5. Prepare it in final form - Check for grammar, punctuation, appearance.

Outline For a Recommendation Report

Is the report:

1. Correct in information, grammar, and tone?
2. Clear?
3. Complete?
4. Concise?
5. Timely?
6. Worth its cost?

Will the report accomplish its purpose?

MANAGEMENT CONTROLS

1. Control

What is control? What is controlled? Who controls?

The essence of control is action which adjusts operations to predetermined standards, and its basis is information in the hands of managers. Control is checking to determine whether plans are being observed and suitable progress toward stated objectives is being made, and action is taken, if necessary, to correct deviations.

We have a ready-made model for this concept of control in the automatic systems which are widely used for process control in the chemical and petroleum industries. A process control system works this way. Suppose, for example, it is desired to maintain a constant rate of flow of oil through a pipe at a predetermined or set-point value. A signal, whose strength represents the rate of flow, can be produced in a measuring device and transmitted to a control mechanism. The control mechanism, when it detects any deviation of the actual from the set-point signal, will reposition the value regulating flow rate.

2. Basis For Control

A process control mechanism thus acts to adjust operations to predetermined standards and does so on the basis of information it receives. In a parallel way, information reaching a manager gives him the opportunity for corrective action and is his basis for control. He cannot exercise control without such information, and he cannot do a complete job of managing without controlling.

3. Policy

What is policy?

Policy is simply a statement of an organization's intention to act in certain ways when specified types of circumstances arise. It represents a general decision, predetermined and expressed as a principle or rule, establishing a normal pattern of conduct for dealing with given types of business events - usually recurrent. A statement is therefore useful in economizing the time of managers and in assisting them to discharge their responsibilities equitably and consistently.

Policy is not a means of control, but policy does generate the need for control.

Adherence to policies is not guaranteed nor can it be taken on faith. It has to be verified. Without verification, there is no basis for control. Policy and procedures, although closely related and interdependent to a certain extent, are not synonymous. A policy may be adopted, for example, to maintain a materials inventory not to exceed one million dollars. A procedure for inventory control would interpret that policy and convert it into methods for keeping within that limit, with consideration, too, of possible but foreseeable expedient deviation.

4. Procedure

What is procedure?

A procedure specifically prescribes:

a. What work is to be performed by the various participants
b. Who are the respective participants
c. When and where the various steps in the different processes are to be performed
d. The sequence of operations that will insure uniform handling of recurring transactions
e. The *paper* that is involved, its origin, transition, and disposition

Necessary appurtenances to a procedure are:

a. Detailed organizational chart

b. Flow charts
c. Exhibits of forms, all presented in close proximity to the text of the procedure

5. Basis of Control - Information in the Hands of Managers
If the basis of control is information in the hands of managers, then reporting is elevated to a level of very considerable importance.

Types of reporting may include:

a. Special reports and routine reports
b. Written, oral, and graphic reports
c. Staff meetings
d. Conferences
e. Television screens
f. Non-receipt of information, as where management is by exception
g. Any other means whereby information is transmitted to a manager as a basis for control action

FRAMEWORK OF MANAGEMENT

Elements

1. Policy - It has to be verified, controlled.

2. Organization - is part of the giving of an assignment. The organizational chart gives to each individual in his title, a first approximation of the nature of his assignment and orients him as being accountable to a certain individual. Organization is not in a true sense a means of control. Control is checking to ascertain whether the assignment is executed as intended and acting on the basis of that information.

3. Budgets - perform three functions:

   a. They present the objectives, plans, and programs of the organization in financial terms.
   b. They report the progress of actual performance against these predetermined objectives, plans, and programs.
   c. Like organizational charts, delegations of authority, procedures and job descriptions, they define the assignments which have flowed from the Chief Executive. Budgets are a means of control in the respect that they report progress of actual performance against the program. They provide information which enables managers to take action directed toward bringing actual results into conformity with the program.

4. Internal Check - provides in practice for the principle that the same person should not have responsibility for all phases of a transaction. This makes it clearly an aspect of organization rather than of control. Internal Check is static, or built-in.

5. Plans, Programs, Objectives
People must know what they are trying to do. Objectives fulfill this need. Without them, people may work industriously and yet, working aimlessly, accomplish little.

Plans and Programs complement Objectives, since they propose how and according to what time schedule the objectives are to be reached.

6. Delegations of Authority
   Among the ways we have for supplementing the titles and lines of authority of an organizational chart are delegations of authority. Delegations of authority clarify the extent of authority of individuals and in that way serve to define assignments. That they are not means of control is apparent from the very fact that wherever there has been a delegation of authority, the need for control increases. This could hardly be expected to happen if delegations of authority were themselves means of control.

Manager's Responsibility

Control becomes necessary whenever a manager delegates authority to a subordinate because he cannot delegate and then simply sit back and forget all about it. A manager's accountability to his own superior has not diminished one whit as a result of delegating part of his authority to a subordinate. The manager must exercise control over actions taken under the authority so delegated. That means checking serves as a basis for possible corrective action.

Objectives, plans, programs, organizational charts, and other elements of the managerial system are not fruitfully regarded as either controls or means of control. They are pre-established standards or models of performance to which operations are adjusted by the exercise of management control. These standards or models of performance are dynamic in character for they are constantly altered, modified, or revised. Policies, organizational set-up, procedures, delegations, etc. are constantly altered but, like objectives and plans, they remain in force until they are either abandoned or revised. All of the elements (or standards or models of performance), objectives, plans and prpgrams, policies, organization, etc. can be regarded as a *framework of management.*

Control Techniques

Examples of control techniques:
1. Compare against established standards
2. Compare with a similar operation
3. Compare with past operations
4. Compare with predictions of accomplishment

Where Forecasts Fit

Control is after-the-fact while forecasts are before. Forecasts and projections are important for setting objectives and formulating plans.

Information for aiming and planning does not have to before-the-fact. It may be an after-the-fact analysis proving that a certain policy has been impolitic in its effect on the relation of the company or department with customer, employee, taxpayer, or stockholder; or that a certain plan is no longer practical, or that a certain procedure is unworkable.

The prescription here certainly would not be in control (in these cases, control would simply bring operations into conformity with obsolete standards) but the establishment of new standards, a new policy, a new plan, and a new procedure to be controlled too.

<u>Information</u> is, of course, the basis for all <u>communication</u> in addition to furnishing evidence to management of the need for reconstructing the framework of management.

PROBLEM SOLVING

The accepted concept in modern management for problem solving is the utilization of the following steps:

1. Identify the problem
2. Gather data
3. List possible solutions
4. Test possible solutions
5. Select the best solution
6. Put the solution into actual practice

Occasions might arise where you would have to apply the second step of gathering data before completing the first step.

You might also find that it will be necessary to work on several steps at the same time.

1. <u>Identify the Problem</u>

Your first step is to define as precisely as possible the problem to be solved. While this may sound easy, it is often the most difficult part of the process.

It has been said of problem solving that you are halfway to the solution when you can write out a clear statement of the problem itself.

Our job now is to get below the surface manifestations of the trouble and pinpoint the problem. This is usually accomplished by a logical analysis, by going from the general to the particular; from the obvious to the not-so-obvious cause.
Let us say that production is behind schedule. WHY? Absenteeism is high. Now, is absenteeism the basic problem to be tackled, or is it merely a symptom of low morale among the workforce? Under these circumstances, you may decide that production is not the problem; the problem is *employee morale.*

In trying to define the problem, remember there is seldom one simple reason why production is lagging, or reports are late, etc.

Analysis usually leads to the discovery that an apparent problem is really made up of several subproblems which must be attacked separately.

Another way is to limit the problem, and thereby ease the task of finding a solution, and concentrate on the elements which are within the scope of your control.

When you have gone this far, write out a tentative statement of the problem to be solved.

2. Gather Data

In the second step, you must set out to collect all the information that might have a bearing on the problem. Do not settle for an assumption when reasonable fact and figures are available.

If you merely go through the motions of problem-solving, you will probably shortcut the information-gathering step. Therefore, do not stack the evidence by confining your research to your own preconceived ideas.

As you collect facts, organize them in some form that helps you make sense of them and spot possible relationships between them. For example: Plotting cost per unit figures on a graph can be more meaningful than a long column of figures.

Evaluate each item as you go along. Is the source material: absolutely reliable, probably reliable, or not to be trusted.

One of the best methods for gathering data is to go out and look the situation over carefully. Talk to the people on the job who are most affected by this problem.

Always keep in mind that a primary source is usually better than a secondary source of information.

3. List Possible Solutions

This is the creative thinking step of problem solving. This is a good time to bring into play whatever techniques of group dynamics the agency or bureau might have developed for a joint attack on problems.

Now the important thing for you to do is: Keep an open mind. Let your imagination roam freely over the facts you have collected. Jot down every possible solution that occurs to you. Resist the temptation to evaluate various proposals as you go along. List seemingly absurd ideas along with more plausible ones. The more possibilities you list during this step, the less risk you will run of settling for merely a workable, rather than the best, solution.

Keep studying the data as long as there seems to be any chance of deriving additional - ideas, solutions, explanations, or patterns from it.

4. Test Possible Solutions

Now you begin to evaluate the possible solutions. Take pains to be objective. Up to this point, you have suspended judgment but you might be tempted to select a solution you secretly favored all along and proclaim it as the best of the lot.

The secret of objectivity in this phase is to test the possible solutions separately, measuring each against a common yardstick. To make this yardstick try to enumerate as many specific criteria as you can think of. Criteria are best phrased as questions which you ask of each possible solution. They can be drawn from these general categories:

Suitability - Will this solution do the job?
Will it solve the problem completely or partially?

Is it a permanent or a stopgap solution?

Feasibility - Will this plan work in actual practice?
Can we afford this approach?
How much will it cost?

Acceptability - Will the boss go along with the changes required in the plan?
Are we trying to drive a tack with a sledge hammer?

5. Select the Best Solution

This is the area of executive decision.

Occasionally, one clearly superior solution will stand out at the conclusion of the testing process. But often it is not that simple. You may find that no one solution has come through all the tests with flying colors.

You may also find that a proposal, which flunked miserably on one of the essential tests, racked up a very high score on others.

The best solution frequently will turn out to be a combination.

Try to arrange a marriage that will bring together the strong points of one possible solution with the particular virtues of another. The more skill and imagination that you apply, the greater is the likelihood that you will come out with a solution that is not merely adequate and workable, but is the best possible under the circumstances.

6. Put the Solution Into Actual Practice

As every executive knows, a plan which works perfectly on paper may develop all sorts of bugs when put into actual practice.

Problem-solving does not stop with selecting the solution which looks best in theory. The next step is to put the chosen solution into action and watch the results. The results may point towards modifications.

If the problem disappears when you put your solution into effect, you know you have the right solution.

If it does not disappear, even after you have adjusted your plan to cover unforeseen difficulties that turned up in practice, work your way back through the problem-solving solutions.

Would one of them have worked better?
Did you overlook some vital piece of data which would have given you a different slant on the whole situation? Did you apply all necessary criteria in testing solutions? If no light dawns after this much rechecking, it is a pretty good bet that you defined the problem incorrectly in the first place.

You came up with the wrong solution because you tackled the wrong problem.

Thus, step six may become step one of a new problem-solving cycle.

COMMUNICATION

1. What is Communication?
   We communicate through writing, speaking, action or inaction. In speaking to people face-to-face, there is opportunity to judge reactions and to adjust the message. This makes the supervisory chain one of the most, and in many instances the most, important channels of communication.

   In an organization, communication means keeping employees informed about the organization's objectives, policies, problems, and progress. Communication is the free interchange of information, ideas, and desirable attitudes between and among employees and between employees and management.

2. Why is Communication Needed?
   a. People have certain social needs
   b. Good communication is essential in meeting those social needs
   c. While people have similar basic needs, at the same time they differ from each other
   d. Communication must be adapted to these individual differences

   An employee cannot do his best work unless he knows why he is doing it. If he has the feeling that he is being kept in the dark about what is going on, his enthusiasm and productivity suffer.

   Effective communication is needed in an organization so that employees will understand what the organization is trying to accomplish; and how the work of one unit contributes to or affects the work of other units in the organization and other organizations.

3. How is Communication Achieved?
   Communication flows downward, upward, sideways.

   a. Communication may come from top management down to employees. This is downward communication.

      Some means of downward communication are:
      (1) Training (orientation, job instruction, supervision, public relations, etc.)
      (2) Conferences
      (3) Staff meetings
      (4) Policy statements
      (5) Bulletins
      (6) Newsletters
      (7) Memoranda
      (8) Circulation of important letters

      In downward communication, it is important that employees be informed in advance of changes that will affect them.

   b. Communications should also be developed so that the ideas, suggestions, and knowledge of employees will flow upward to top management.

Some means of upward communication are:

(1) Personal discussion conferences
(2) Committees
(3) Memoranda
(4) Employees suggestion program
(5) Questionnaires to be filled in giving comments and suggestions about proposed actions that will affect field operations

Upward communication requires that management be willing to listen, to accept, and to make changes when good ideas are present. Upward communication succeeds when there is no fear of punishment for speaking out or lack of interest at the top. Employees will share their knowledge and ideas with management when interest is shown and recognition is given.

c. The *advantages* of downward communication:
   (1) It enables the passing down of orders, policies, and plans necessary to the continued operation of the station.
   (2) By making information available, it diminishes the fears and suspicions which result from misinformation and misunderstanding.
   (3) It fosters the pride people want to have in their work when they are told of good work.
   (4) It improves the morale and stature of the individual to be *in the know.*
   (5) It helps employees to understand, accept, and cooperate with changes when they know about them in advance.

d. The *advantages* of upward communication:
   (1) It enables the passing upward of information, attitudes, and feelings.
   (2) It makes it easier to find out how ready people are to receive downward communication.
   (3) It reveals the degree to which the downward communication is understood and accepted.
   (4) It helps to satisfy the basic *social* needs.
   (5) It stimulates employees to participate in the operation of their organization.
   (6) It encourages employees to contribute ideas for improving the efficiency and economy of operations.
   (7) It helps to solve problem situations before they reach the explosion point.

4. Why Does Communication Fail?
   a. The technical difficulties of conveying information clearly
   b. The emotional content of communication which prevents complete transmission
   c. The fact that there is a difference between what management needs to say, what it wants to say, and what it does say
   d. The fact that there is a difference between what employees would like to say, what they think is profitable or safe to say, and what they do say

5. How to Improve Communication.
   As a supervisor, you are a key figure in communication. To improve as a communicator, you should:
   a. Know - Knowing your subordinates will help you to recognize and work with individual differences.

b. Like - If you like those who work for you and those for whom you work, this will foster the kind of friendly, warm, work atmosphere that will facilitate communication.
c. Trust - Showing a sincere desire to communicate will help to develop the mutual trust and confidence which are essential to the free flow of communication.
d. Tell - Tell your subordinates and superiors *what's doing*. Tell your subordinates *why* as well as *how*.
e. Listen - By listening, you help others to talk and you create good listeners. Don't forget that listening implies action.
f. Stimulate - Communication has to be stimulated and encouraged. Be receptive to ideas and suggestions and motivate your people so that each member of the team identifies himself with the job at hand.
g. Consult - The most effective way of consulting is to let your people participate, insofar as possible, in developing determinations which affect them or their work.

6. How to Determine Whether You are Getting Across.
   a. Check to see that communication is received and understood
   b. Judge this understanding by actions rather than words
   c. Adapt or vary communication, when necessary
   d. Remember that good communication cannot cure all problems

7. The Key Attitude.
   Try to see things from the other person's point of view. By doing this, you help to develop the permissive atmosphere and the shared confidence and understanding which are essential to effective two-way communication.

   Communication is a two-way process.
   a. The basic purpose of any communication is to get action.
   b. The only way to get action is through acceptance.
   c. In order to get acceptance, communication must be humanly satisfying as well as technically efficient.

HOW ORDERS AND INSTRUCTIONS SHOULD BE GIVEN

Characteristics of Good Orders and Instructions

1. Clear
   Orders should be definite as to
   - What is to be done
   - Who is to do it
   - When it is to be done
   - Where it is to be done
   - How it is to be done

2. Concise
   Avoid wordiness. Orders should be brief and to the point.

3. Timely
   Instructions and orders should be sent out at the proper time and not too long in advance of expected performance.

4. Possibility of Performance
   Orders should be feasible:
   a. Investigate before giving orders
   b. Consult those who are to carry out instructions before formulating and issuing them

5. Properly Directed
   Give the orders to the people concerned. Do not send orders to people who are not concerned. People who continually receive instructions that are not applicable to them get in the habit of neglecting instructions generally.

6. Reviewed Before Issuance
   Orders should be reviewed before issuance:
   a. Test them by putting yourself in the position of the recipient
   b. If they involve new procedures, have the persons who are to do the work review them for suggestions

7. Reviewed After Issuance
   Persons who receive orders should be allowed to raise questions and to point out unforeseen consequences of orders.

8. Coordinated
   Orders should be coordinated so that work runs smoothly.

9. Courteous
   Make a request rather than a demand. There is no need to continually call attention to the fact that you are the boss.

10. Recognizable as an Order
    Be sure that the order is recognizable as such.

11. Complete
    Be sure recipient has knowledge and experience sufficient to carry out order. Give illustrations and examples.

A DEPARTMENTAL PERSONNEL OFFICE IS RESPONSIBLE FOR THE FOLLOWING FUNCTIONS

1. Policy
2. Personnel Programs
3. Recruitment and Placement
4. Position Classification
5. Salary and Wage Administration
6. Employee Performance Standards and Evaluation
7. Employee Relations
8. Disciplinary Actions and Separations
9. Health and Safety
10. Staff Training and Development
11. Personnel Records, Procedures, and Reports
12. Employee Services
13. Personnel Research

23

SUPERVISION

Leadership

All leadership is based essentially on authority. This comes from two sources: it is received from higher management or it is earned by the supervisor through his methods of supervision. Although effective leadership has always depended upon the leader's using his authority in such a way as to appeal successfully to the motives of the people supervised, the conditions for making this appeal are continually changing. The key to today's problem of leadership is flexibility and resourcefulness on the part of the leader in meeting changes in conditions as they occur.

Three basic approaches to leadership are generally recognized:

1. The Authoritarian Approach
   a. The methods and techniques used in this approach emphasize the *I* in leadership and depend primarily on the formal authority of the leader. This authority is sometimes exercised in a hardboiled manner and sometimes in a benevolent manner, but in either case the dominating role of the leader is reflected in the thinking, planning, and decisions of the group.
   b. Group results are to a large degree dependent on close supervision by the leader. Usually, the individuals in the group will not show a high degree of initiative or acceptance of responsibility and their capacity to grow and develop probably will not be fully utilized. The group may react with resentment or submission, depending upon the manner and skill of the leader in using his authority
   c. This approach develops as a natural outgrowth of the authority that goes with the leader's job and his feeling of sole responsibility for getting the job done. It is relatively easy to use and does not require much resourcefulness.
   d. The use of this approach is effective in times of emergencies, in meeting close deadlines as a final resort, in settling some issues, in disciplinary matters, and with dependent individuals and groups.

2. The Laissez-Faire or *Let 'em Alone* Approach
   a. This approach generally is characterized by an avoidance of leadership responsibility by the leader. The activities of the group depend largely on the choice of its members rather than the leader.
   b. Group results probably will be poor. Generally, there will be disagreements over petty things, bickering, and confusion. Except for a few aggressive people, individuals will not show much initiative and growth and development will be retarded. There may be a tendency for informal leaders to take over leadership of the group.
   c. This approach frequently results from the leader's dislike of responsibility, from his lack of confidence, from failure of other methods to work, from disappointment or criticism. It is usually the easiest of the three to use and requires both understanding and resourcefulness on the part of the leader.
   d. This approach is occasionally useful and effective, particularly in forcing dependent individuals or groups to rely on themselves, to give someone a chance to save face by clearing his own difficulties, or when action should be delayed temporarily for good cause.

3. The Democratic Approach
   a. The methods and techniques used in this approach emphasize the *we* in leadership and build up the responsibility of the group to attain its objectives. Reliance is placed largely on the earned authority of the leader.
   b. Group results are likely to be good because most of the job motives of the people will be satisfied. Cooperation and teamwork, initiative, acceptance of responsibility, and the individual's capacity for growth probably will show a high degree of development.
   c. This approach grows out of a desire or necessity of the leader to find ways to appeal effectively to the motivation of his group. It is the best approach to build up inside the person a strong desire to cooperate and apply himself to the job.
      It is the most difficult to develop, and requires both understanding and resourcefulness on the part of the leader.
   d. The value of this approach increases over a long period where sustained efficiency and development of people are important. It may not be fully effective in all situations, however, particularly when there is not sufficient time to use it properly or where quick decisions must be made.

All three approaches are used by most leaders and have a place in supervising people. The extent of their use varies with individual leaders, with some using one approach predominantly. The leader who uses these three approaches, and varies their use with time and circumstance, is probably the most effective. Leadership which is used predominantly with a democratic approach requires more resourcefulness on the part of the leader but offers the greatest possibilities in terms of teamwork and cooperation.

The one best way of developing democratic leadership is to provide a real sense of participation on the part of the group, since this satisfies most of the chief job motives. Although there are many ways of providing participation, consulting as frequently as possible with individuals and groups on things that affect them seems to offer the most in building cooperation and responsibility. Consultation takes different forms, but it is most constructive when people feel they are actually helping in finding the answers to the problems on the job.

There are some requirements of leaders in respect to human relations which should be considered in their selection and development. Generally, the leader should be interested in working with other people, emotionally stable, self-confident, and sensitive to the reactions of others. In addition, his viewpoint should be one of getting the job done through people who work cooperatively in response to his leadership. He should have a knowledge of individual and group behavior, but, most important of all, he should work to combine all of these requirements into a definite, practical skill in leadership.

Nine Points of Contrast Between *Boss* and *Leader*

1. The boss drives his men; the leader coaches them.
2. The boss depends on authority; the leader on good will.
3. The boss inspires fear; the leader inspires enthusiasm.
4. The boss says J; the leader says *We*.
5. The boss says *Get here on time;* the leader gets there ahead of time.
6. The boss fixes the blame for the breakdown; the leader fixes the breakdown.
7. The boss knows how it is done; the leader shows how.
8. The boss makes work a drudgery; the leader makes work a game.
9. The boss says *Go*; the leader says *Let's go.*

EMPLOYEE MORALE

Employee morale is the way employees feel about each other, the organization or unit in which they work, and the work they perform.

Some Ways to Develop and Maintain Good Employee Morale

1. Give adequate credit and praise when due.
2. Recognize importance of all jobs and equalize load with proper assignments, always giving consideration to personality differences and abilities.
3. Welcome suggestions and do not have an *all-wise* attitude. Request employees' assistance in solving problems and use assistants when conducting group meetings on certain subjects.
4. Properly assign responsibilities and give adequate authority for fulfillment of such assignments.
5. Keep employees informed about matters that affect them.
6. Criticize and reprimand employees privately.
7. Be accessible and willing to listen.
8. Be fair.
9. Be alert to detect training possibilities so that you will not miss an opportunity to help each employee do a better job, and if possible with less effort on his part.
10. Set a good example.
11. Apply the golden rule.

Some Indicators of Good Morale

1. Good quality of work
2. Good quantity
3. Good attitude of employees
4. Good discipline
5. Teamwork
6. Good attendance
7. Employee participation

MOTIVATION

Drives

A *drive,* stated simply, is a desire or force which causes a person to do or say certain things. These are some of the most usual drives and some of their identifying characteristics recognizable in people motivated by such drives:

1. Security (desire to provide for the future)
   Always on time for work
   Works for the same employer for many years
   Never takes unnecessary chances Seldom resists doing what he is told

2. Recognition (desire to be rewarded for accomplishment)
   Likes to be asked for his opinion
   Becomes very disturbed when he makes a mistake
   Does things to attract attention

Likes to see his name in print

3. <u>Position</u> (desire to hold certain status in relation to others)
   Boasts about important people he knows
   Wants to be known as a key man
   Likes titles
   Demands respect
   Belongs to clubs, for prestige

4. <u>Accomplishment</u> (desire to get things done)
   Complains when things are held up
   Likes to do things that have tangible results
   Never lies down on the job
   Is proud of turning out good work

5. <u>Companionship</u> (desire to associate with other people)
   Likes to work with others
   Tells stories and jokes
   Indulges in horseplay
   Finds excuses to talk to others on the job

6. <u>Possession</u> (desire to collect and hoard objects)
   Likes to collect things
   Puts his name on things belonging to him
   Insists on the same work location

Supervisors may find that identifying the drives of employees is a helpful step toward motivating them to self-improvement and better job performance. For example: An employee's job performance is below average. His supervisor, having previously determined that the employee is motivated by a drive for security, suggests that taking training courses will help the employee to improve, advance, and earn more money. Since earning more money can be a step toward greater security, the employee's drive for security would motivate him to take the training suggested by the supervisor. In essence, this is the process of charting an employee's future course by using his motivating drives to positive advantage.

EMPLOYEE PARTICIPATION

What is Participation?

Employee participation is the employee's giving freely of his time, skill and knowledge to an extent which cannot be obtained by demand.

Why is it Important?

The supervisor's responsibility is to get the job done through people. A good supervisor gets the job done through people who work willingly and well. The participation of employees is important because:

1. Employees develop a greater sense of responsibility when they share in working out operating plans and goals.
2. Participation provides greater opportunity and stimulation for employees to learn, and to develop their ability.

3. Participation sometimes provides better solutions to problems because such solutions may combine the experience and knowledge of interested employees who want the solutions to work.
4. An employee or group may offer a solution which the supervisor might hesitate to make for fear of demanding too much.
5. Since the group wants to make the solution work, they exert *pressure* in a constructive way on each other.
6. Participation usually results in reducing the need for close supervision.

How May Supervisors Obtain It?

Participation is encouraged when employees feel that they share some responsibility for the work and that their ideas are sincerely wanted and valued. Some ways of obtaining employee participation are:

1. Conduct orientation programs for new employees to inform them about the organization and their rights and responsibilities as employees.
2. Explain the aims and objectives of the agency. On a continuing basis, be sure that the employees know what these aims and objectives are.
3. Share job successes and responsibilities and give credit for success.
4. Consult with employees, both as individuals and in groups, about things that affect them.
5. Encourage suggestions for job improvements. Help employees to develop good suggestions. The suggestions can bring them recognition. The city's suggestion program offers additional encouragement through cash awards.

The supervisor who encourages employee participation is not surrendering his authority. He must still make decisions and initiate action, and he must continue to be ultimately responsible for the work of those he supervises. But, through employee participation, he is helping his group to develop greater ability and a sense of responsibility while getting the job done faster and better.

STEPS IN HANDLING A GRIEVANCE

1. Get the facts
   a. Listen sympathetically.
   b. Let him talk himself out.
   c. Get his story straight.
   d. Get his point of view.
   e. Don't argue with him.
   f. Give him plenty of time.
   g. Conduct the interview privately.
   h. Don't try to shift the blame or pass the buck.

2. Consider the facts
   a. Consider the employee's viewpoint.
   b. How will the decision affect similar cases.
   c. Consider each decision as a possible precedent.
   d. Avoid snap judgments - don't jump to conclusions.

3. Make or get a decision
   a. Frame an effective counter-proposal.
   b. Make sure it is fair to all.
   c. Have confidence in your judgment.
   d. Be sure you can substantiate your decision.

4. Notify the employee of your decision
   Be sure he is told; try to convince him that the decision is fair and just.

5. Take action when needed and if within your authority
   Otherwise, tell employee that the matter will be called to the attention of the proper person or that nothing can be done, and why it cannot.

6. Follow through to see that the desired result is achieved.

7. Record key facts concerning the complaint and the action taken.

8. Leave the way open to him to appeal your decision to a higher authority.

9. Report all grievances to your superior, whether they are appealed or not.

DISCIPLINE

Discipline is training that develops self-control, orderly conduct, and efficiency.

To discipline does not necessarily mean to punish.

To discipline does mean to train, to regulate, and to govern conduct.

The Disciplinary Interview

Most employees sincerely want to do what is expected of them. In other words, they are self-disciplined. Some employees, however, fail to observe established rules and standards, and disciplinary action by the supervisor is required.

The primary purpose of disciplinary action is to improve conduct without creating dissatisfaction, bitterness, or resentment in the process.

Constructive disciplinary action is more concerned with causes and explanations of breaches of conduct than with punishment. The disciplinary interview is held to get at the causes of apparent misbehavior and to motivate better performance in the future.

It is important that the interview be kept on as impersonal a basis as possible. If the supervisor lets the interview descend to the plane of an argument, it loses its effectiveness.

Planning the Interview

Get all pertinent facts concerning the situation so that you can talk in specific terms to the employee.

Review the employee's record, appraisal ratings, etc.

Consider what you know about the temperament of the employee. Consider your attitude toward the employee. Remember that the primary requisite of disciplinary action is fairness.

Don't enter upon the interview when angry.

Schedule the interview for a place which is private and out of hearing of others.

Conducting the Interview

1. Make an effort to establish accord.

2. Question the employee about the apparent breach of discipline. Be sure that the question is not so worded as to be itself an accusation.

3. Give the employee a chance to tell his side of the story. Give him ample opportunity to talk.

4. Use understanding-listening except where it is necessary to ask a question or to point out some details of which the employee may not be aware. If the employee misrepresents facts, make a plain, accurate statement of the facts, but don't argue and don't engage in personal controversy.

5. Listen and try to understand the reasons for the employee's (mis)conduct. First of all, don't assume that there has been a breach of discipline. Evaluate the employee's reasons for his conduct in the light of his opinions and feelings concerning the consistency and reasonableness of the standards which he was expected to follow. Has the supervisor done his part in explaining the reasons for the rules? Was the employee's behavior unintentional or deliberate? Does he think he had real reasons for his actions? What new facts is he telling? Do the facts justify his actions? What causes, other than those mentioned, could have stimulated the behavior?

6. After listening to the employee's version of the situation, and if censure of his actions is warranted, the supervisor should proceed with whatever criticism is justified. Emphasis should be placed on future improvement rather than exclusively on the employee's failure to measure up to expected standards of job conduct.

7. Fit the criticism to the individual. With one employee, a word of correction may be all that is required.

8. Attempt to distinguish between unintentional error and deliberate misbehavior. An error due to ignorance requires training and not censure.

9. Administer criticism in a controlled, even tone of voice, never in anger. Make it clear that you are acting as an agent of the department. In general, criticism should refer to the job or the employee's actions and not to the person. Criticism of the employee's work is not an attack on the individual.

30

10. Be sure the interview does not destroy the employee's self-confidence. Mention his good qualities and assure him that you feel confident that he can improve his performance.
11. Wherever possible, before the employee leaves the interview, satisfy him that the incident is closed, that nothing more will be said on the subject unless the offense is repeated.

CPSIA information can be obtained
at www.ICGtesting.com
Printed in the USA
LVHW062334271019
635513LV00005B/129/P